American Mosaic

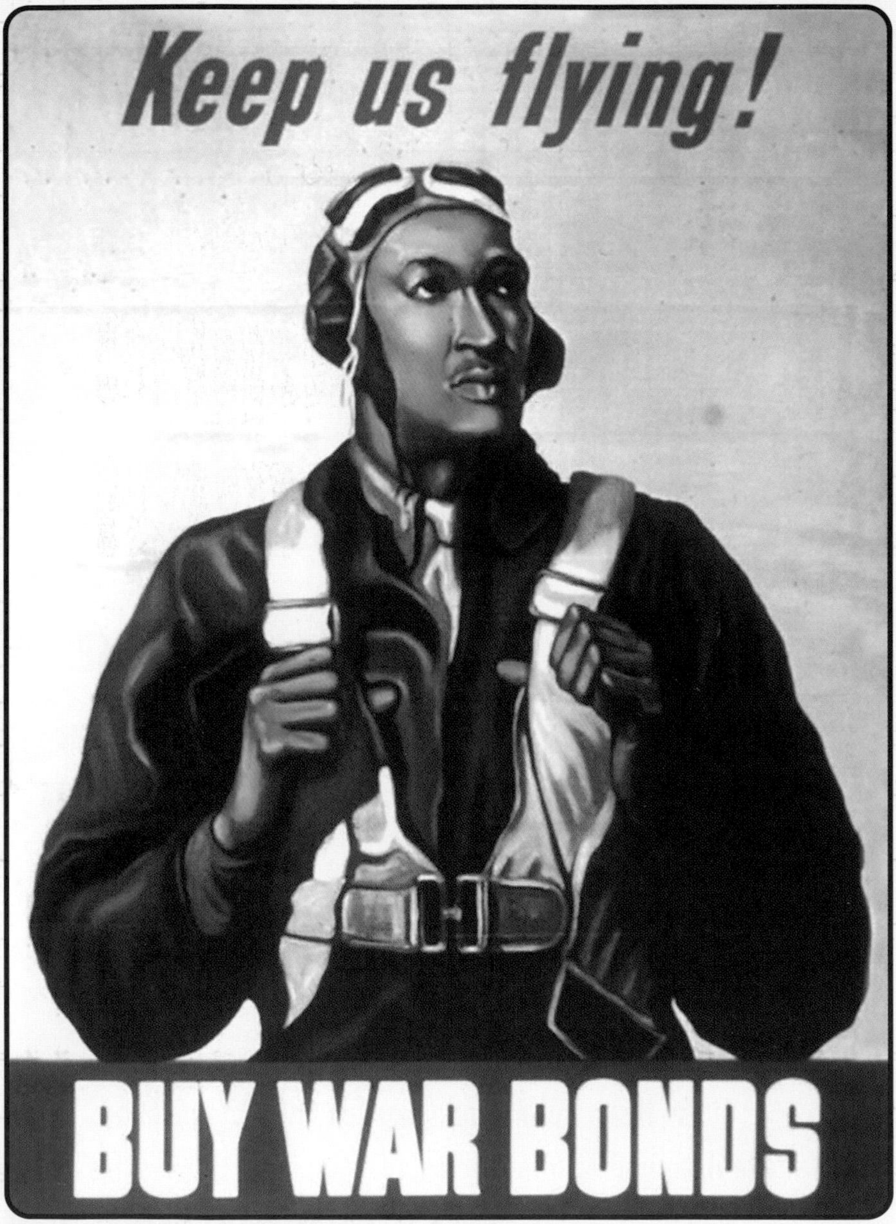
Keep us flying!
BUY WAR BONDS

American Mosaic

AFRICAN-AMERICAN CONTRIBUTIONS

The Tuskegee Airmen

Judy L. Hasday

CHELSEA HOUSE
P U B L I S H E R S

A Haights Cross Communications Company

Philadelphia

Frontis: A War Bonds poster featuring a Tuskegee Airman from 1942.

Dedication: This one's for you Ben, with love. I hope you learn to develop the same perseverance, determination, and integrity as the men whose story is told within these pages.

CHELSEA HOUSE PUBLISHERS

VP, NEW PRODUCT DEVELOPMENT Sally Cheney
DIRECTOR OF PRODUCTION Kim Shinners
CREATIVE MANAGER Takeshi Takahashi
MANUFACTURING MANAGER Diann Grasse

Staff for TUSKEGEE AIRMEN

ASSOCIATE EDITOR Benjamin Xavier Kim
PRODUCTION EDITOR Jaimie Winkler
PICTURE RESEARCHER Pat Holl
COVER AND SERIES DESIGNER Keith Trego
LAYOUT 21st Century Publishing and Communications, Inc.

http://www.chelseahouse.com

First Printing

1 3 5 7 9 8 6 4 2

Library of Congress Cataloging-in-Publication Data

Hasday, Judy L., 1957–
   The Tuskegee airmen / by Judy Hasday.
      p. cm. — (American mosaic)
Includes index.
   ISBN 0-7910-7267-3
   1. World War, 1939–1945—Participation, African American—Juvenile literature. 2. United States. Army Air Forces. Fighter Squadron, 99th—History—Juvenile literature. 3. African American air pilots—History—Juvenile literature. 4. World War, 1939–1945—Aerial operations, American—Juvenile literature. 5. Tuskegee Army Air Field (Ala.)—Juvenile literature. 6. World War, 1939–1945—Campaigns—Western Front—Juvenile literature. 7. World War, 1939–1945—Regimental histories—United States—Juvenile literature. I. Title. II. Series.
D810.N4 H37 2002
940.54'4973—dc21
                                        2002152058

Table of Contents

The efforts of blacks in times of warfare in America date to colonial times. Massachusetts slave Peter Salem (shown here) participated in the Battle of Bunker Hill, one of the first conflicts of the Revolutionary War.

The Right
to Fight

"I expected much of you . . . but you surpassed my hopes."

—General Andrew Jackson to his black
militia company, War of 1812

From the Revolutionary War to the current war on terrorism, African Americans have taken up arms to defend America from its enemies. The upper echelons of the American military service, however, have not always welcomed their support. It was bad enough that African Americans had to endure the virulent racism that ran unchecked in the private sector, where school segregation was permitted and unfair employment practices were rampant, to say nothing of the public humiliation suffered by having to use separate streetcars, water fountains, and restaurants.

Despite the racism and ill treatment they have endured since being brought to the shores of North America as slaves, African–American soldiers have taken up arms to fight for this country since the Revolutionary War. As early as the days when Europeans began colonizing the New World, blacks have been a part of America's development. Though not initially permitted to carry arms, in 1641 blacks were issued tomahawks to assist settlers in fighting off Indian attacks in New Amsterdam. According to military scholar Richard M. Dalfiume, colonial leaders were happy to arm blacks "when emergencies, such as Indian threats, arose and there was an immediate need for manpower." Slaves and free blacks were called upon to help defend forts, outposts, and settlements during a crisis. However, when the threat ended, the blacks were disarmed and most were restricted from serving in a peacetime militia.

For a while, free blacks were permitted to enlist in a militia. In 1711 they fought in the Tuscarora War; in 1715 they fought in the Yamassee War. In 1730, blacks fought for the French against the Natchez Indians in Louisiana. When a Spanish force was assembled to fight the Natchez in Mobile, Alabama in 1736, a company of blacks, including free blacks serving as officers, joined them in battle. It was the first time blacks served as officers in a military unit. In the French and Indian War, black militia units fought with some of the colonists, and also fought with British forces, serving as scouts, wagoneers, and laborers. Many won honors for their bravery in battle. "Negro Mountain" in Maryland is so named to honor a black soldier killed during a battle with Indians.

When the colonists decided to break away from the British and establish their independence, war broke out. Blacks played a major role in the Revolutionary War, with almost 5,000 of them serving in various capacities in the war effort. The colonists only allowed free blacks to fight, but the British began offering freedom to slaves to fight with the King's troops. They formed the "Ethiopian Regiment" and wore the inscription "Liberty to Slaves" on their uniforms. General George Washington preferred not to have blacks serve in the Continental Army, but as the Americans suffered casualties, he relented, as the need for more soldiers increased.

Though countless black soldiers fought bravely, most died unknown. Some of their heroics did manage to make it into military records. Massachusetts slave Peter Salem was at the Battle of Bunker Hill, firing one of the shots "heard 'round the world." Prince Whipple was with Washington's army when they crossed the Delaware. James Armistead played an important role as a spy for the Americans. He waited on Lord Cornwallis' table at Yorktown and passed on information about any military plans he heard Cornwallis discuss. Blacks also served in the Continental Navy. Nearly one-fourth of all American seamen were black.

Despite the contributions by African Americans in the Revolutionary War, most were removed from the military once the war ended. Many had been honored for their courageous service and had been awarded medals. The most shameful irony was that many of the blacks who fought with the colonists for independence from the British were re-enslaved. More humiliation followed when, in 1792, the new United States Congress passed an act that restricted future military service to "free able-bodied white male citizens." The Marine Corps followed the same policy when it was established in 1798. The rules expressly stated that "no Negro, mulatto or Indian" would be allowed to enlist. The country that was founded on the belief of "life, liberty and the pursuit of happiness" for all did not extend those very same rights to the blacks who fought and died to defend her.

In the newly formed United States of America, the practice of owning slaves resumed, particularly in the southern states. A slave's life was a bleak existence. Mistreated and ill-fed, black slaves were forced to work long, difficult hours harvesting crops and relegated to handle much of the menial day-to-day labor on their masters' properties. Famed explorers Meriweather Lewis and William Clark brought a brawny young slave named York with them on their 1804–5 journey through the Louisiana Territory.

Slaves were not paid any wages, had no legal rights, and could be bought and sold like any other possession.

For twenty years after the Revolutionary War, this was the life of most blacks in America. Then came the War of 1812. Once again the British and the Americans recruited blacks to take up arms and join the battle. Though President James Madison, a Southerner from Virginia, objected to enlisting blacks, General Andrew Jackson issued a request for their services to help defend New Orleans. Six hundred blacks fought alongside Jackson and his white troops, successfully protecting the Louisiana port city.

Though blacks fought in land battles, the War of 1812 was largely a naval war, and many of the experienced blacks who had served in the Continental Navy eagerly joined the sea battles. One of every ten sailors aboard Commodore Perry's ship was black when they "met the enemy" at Lake Erie. After achieving victory Perry said of his black sailors, "They seemed absolutely insensible to danger." Even though black soldiers and sailors received praise for their conduct in battle, things returned to the way they had been before as soon as the war was over. Some blacks who had anticipated being given their freedom were instead returned to their masters.

While Americans may have been weary of war, there were many issues that pitted Northerners against Southerners—not the least of which was the question of slavery. It became one of the root causes of the third major war in a country less than 100 years old. Though initially prohibited from fighting in the Civil War when it broke out in 1861, blacks were finally permitted to take up arms to defend their country once again. On September 22, 1862, President Abraham Lincoln's Emancipation Proclamation officially authorized blacks to enlist in "the armed services of the United States to garrison forts, positions, stations, and other places to man vessels of all sorts in said service." In 1863 the United States Colored Troops (USCT) were created, though all the officers were white.

President Lincoln's Emancipation Proclamation freed slaves and accepted blacks into the armed services. With the creation of the United States Colored Troops (USCT) on May 22, 1863, blacks like the Union Infantry corporal pictured were permitted to take up arms.

The Fifty-Fourth Massachusetts Volunteer Regiment was the first all-black regiment. This was but one of one hundred and seventy formed during the course of the war. Once again, blacks demonstrated their bravery and discipline as military soldiers. Colonel T. W. Higginson, commander of the all-black First South Carolina Union Volunteers wrote in his February 1, 1863 report:

> No officer in this regiment doubts that the key to the successful prosecution of this war lies in the unlimited employment of black troops. Their superiority lies simply in the fact that they know the country, while white troops do not, and, moreover, that they have peculiarities of temperament, position, and motive which belong to them alone. Instead of leaving their homes and families to fight they are fighting for their homes and families, and they show the resolution and sagacity which a personal purpose gives. . . .

In an assault on Fort Wagner, South Carolina, black sergeant Robert Carney, fighting with the Fifty-Fourth Regiment, seized the flag and ran all the way to the entrance gates of the fort. Though shot in the scalp, Wagner later proudly declared, "The flag never touched the ground, boys." Wagner was one of twenty-three black recipients of the Congressional Medal of Honor. As the war was coming to an end, President Lincoln stated, "Negroes have demonstrated with their blood their right to citizenship."

More than 180,000 blacks served in USCT units. If spies, medical teams, and volunteers in state units were added in, close to 390,000 blacks—about 10 percent of the Union Army—fought in the Civil War. By 1865, more than 37,000 black soldiers had died, or almost 35 percent of the total number of blacks who served in combat. Ironically, after General William Tecumseh Sherman recommended that the military become integrated, both the army and navy rejected the suggestion.

After the Civil War, Congress authorized the formation of six black troop regiments, two of cavalry and four of infantry. For more than twenty years, the Ninth and Tenth Cavalry Regiments, under the commands of Colonel Edward Hatch and Colonel Benjamin Grierson respectively, were assigned to the western frontier from Montana to Texas, including New Mexico, Arizona, Colorado, and the Dakotas. These black soldiers, some who were former

Black cavalry soldiers who fought on the western frontier were nicknamed "Buffalo Soldiers" by the Native Americans because of their tightly curled hair and out of respect for their fighting spirit.

slaves, served to protect settlers, farmers, stagecoach, mail, and railroad crews. They also constructed forts, strung telegraph lines, and built roads.

The black cavalry soldiers often engaged in battles with many Indian tribes, including the Comanche, Kiowa, Arapahoe, Cheyenne, and Apache. The Indians nicknamed the black cavalrymen "Buffalo Soldiers" because of their tightly curled hair and their strong spirit and bravery (buffalo are highly esteemed by Native Americans). The black soldiers accepted the nickname proudly. In fact, the Tenth Cavalry Regiment liked it so much they incorporated the image of the buffalo as part of their insignia.

Often left to fulfill their duties with inadequate ammunition or weapons, old equipment and clothing, and the worst horses, the Buffalo Soldiers maintained high morale—they had the lowest desertion rate of any army unit. They battled two of the fiercest

Apache Indian chiefs, Victorio and Geronimo, and helped bring order back to lawless towns like Lincoln, New Mexico, where bandits like Billy the Kid roamed wild. Several members of the Ninth and Tenth Cavalries were awarded Congressional Medals of Honor.

Despite countless acts of bravery, praise from their white commanders, and willingness to serve their country, black soldiers were still not treated as equals. When the battleship *Maine* was sunk in Havana harbor in 1898 (an event that triggered the start of the Spanish-American War), 22 black sailors died with the rest of the crew. When the Tenth Cavalry arrived in Florida to board military ships that would take them to Cuba to fight yet another war for America, they were segregated from the white soldiers. Conditions were deplorable. Twenty-Fifth Regiment Sergeant Frank Pullen described their quarters, recalling, "There was no light, except the small portholes when the gangplank was closed. So dark was it that candles were burned all day. There was no air except what came down the canvas air-shafts when they were turned to the breeze. The heat of the place was almost unendurable."

Still, the black soldiers fought bravely and honorably. The Twenty-Fifth Regiment was the first to arrive at El Caney and captured the Spanish flag. However, when the white troops of the Twelfth Regiment arrived later, an officer demanded that they be given the flag. Along with Teddy Roosevelt's "Rough Riders," the black cavalry units joined the charge up San Juan Hill. Again the black soldiers were praised for their actions in battle, and again another six Congressional Medals of Honor were awarded.

Just when it began to look like the United States War Department seemed willing to take another look at their racial policies, the blacks were burdened with a troubling incident. The incident was known as the Brownsville Case of 1906. After serving in the Philippines at the conclusion of the Spanish-American War, the Twenty-Fifth Infantry was recalled to the states. On July 28, 1906, the black soldiers arrived at Fort Brown in Brownsville, Texas. The townspeople were not too welcoming to blacks, and even less hospitable toward black servicemen. Whenever the black soldiers left the fort and went into town, they were openly ridiculed and treated with contempt. Late on the evening of August 13th, a shooting spree erupted, resulting in the death of a white bartender and the wounding of a police officer. Several of the soldiers from the Twenty-Fifth were accused of the crime.

Texas Rangers investigated the case and determined that twelve of the men had been involved. Despite the accusations leveled against them, the men of the Twenty-Fifth pleaded their innocence. The evidence backed up their innocence—their horses were cooled down and rested and inspection of their weapons showed no gun had been fired. Since no other soldiers would testify against the men, no indictments were issued. However, President Theodore Roosevelt, infuriated over the lack of cooperation, gave dishonorable discharges to all 167 members of the Twenty-Fifth Infantry Regiment. The soldiers were stripped of their ranks, and their military pensions and veteran's benefits were revoked.

Among the men who bravely served in the Twenty-Fifth were six Medal of Honor recipients, and thirteen who had been given citations for bravery in the Spanish-American War. Due to an outcry of injustice from various Senate and military investigations of the incident, fourteen of the soldiers were given honorable discharges in 1910. It wasn't until 1972 that the remaining members of the Twenty-Fifth received justice, when President Nixon's administration awarded honorable discharges to all of them.

Given the track record of the military's treatment of blacks in the armed forces, it is surprising that any would want to continue to serve their country. Blacks fared no better outside actual field combat, either. The military academies of West Point (army) and Annapolis (navy) turned a blind eye to the rampant racism within their walls. Of the twenty-two black cadets appointed to West Point from 1870 to 1889, only three made it to graduation. The first graduate was Georgia native Henry O. Flipper. He completed his term in 1877, but was later accused of embezzling government funds and court-martialed. (He was pardoned in 1999 by President Bill Clinton.)

John H. Alexander was the second black graduate from West

An amputee veteran watches a victory parade of the 369th Regiment. The 369th soldiers, nicknamed "Hell Fighters" by the Germans in World War I, "never lost a man captured, a trench, or a foot of ground" during 191 days of battle.

Point, graduating in 1887, but he died just seven years later. In 1884, cadet Charles Young entered West Point. The son of a free black soldier who served in the Union Army during the Civil War, Young endured a lonely existence at the academy, shunned by his white classmates. Though last in his class, Young graduated in 1888. It would be forty years before another black cadet would enter West Point.

After the Brownsville incident, blacks were again eased out of the military. By the time the United States got entangled in World War I, only 3 percent of the military was composed of blacks. But with the call of war they came out to serve again by the hundreds of thousands. Thirty thousand served in combat in France. The men of the 369th Regiment earned the nickname "Hell Fighters" from the Germans for battling in the trenches for 191 days without being captured or retreating. The French awarded the croix de guerre, an award for bravery in war, to the entire regiment.

When the war ended in 1918, black soldiers hoped that they would receive a warm welcome back in the States. But instead of receiving respect and admiration for their efforts, they were greeted with more of the same prejudice and loathing. Animosity between whites and blacks in America was reaching a boiling point, and things finally erupted in the summer of 1919. Race riots broke out in cities across the country. More than seventy blacks were lynched—some of them servicemen still in uniform.

In the period between World War I and World War II, the country was devastated by the Great Depression. Whites were poor, and blacks were destitute. Many whites opted to enlist in the military as a way out of their blight. Blacks, however, were turned away, as the armed forces saw no need for the black soldier in peacetime. When the Army and Navy Air Corps became an integral part of the military, blacks were hopeful that opportunities might open up for them. However, their desire to fly was met with the narrow-minded view that they were not smart enough or capable enough to fly a combat aircraft. To support these beliefs, the War College issued a report in 1925 which stated that blacks were "a subspecies of the human population," and probably "the worst of all races." The report went on to say that in the opinion of the military officials who released their findings, blacks would not make good officers. Most officers implied that blacks would also not be good pilots. It would take some courageous and spirited men and women to prove them wrong.

Wilbur Wright photographs his brother Orville taking a test flight in Fort Meyer, Virginia. The Wrights' pioneering efforts in aviation would inspire both whites and blacks to dream of flying. Many years passed before blacks were allowed to take to the skies.

2

Taking to the Skies

"The color of my skin was a drawback at first. . . . I was a curiosity, but soon the public discovered I could really fly. . . . "

—Bessie Coleman, the first black woman
to earn her pilot's license

The history of blacks in aviation is a story of great sacrifice, strong resolve, and ultimately, success. The United States Department of the Air Force wasn't created until 1947, a full two years after the end of World War II. Prior to that time, flying in the military was a part of the army branch and was called the U.S. Air Corps. Before 1940, no blacks were allowed to enter into military pilot training. Before 1939, no blacks could even receive civilian pilot training, so the skies were not open to blacks. Despite the racial obstacles faced by blacks in America, there were those who still found ways to take to the skies.

Airplane flight was a new invention at the turn of the twentieth century. Wilbur and Orville Wright successfully lifted off in a powered aircraft from Kitty Hawk, North Carolina, on December 17, 1903. A few years later, the first-known American black pilot, Eugene Jacques Bullard, flew over the war skies of Europe during World War I. He was one of the greatest American flying aces during the war, but never flew for his native country. Bullard flew as a member of the French Air Service, piloting the skies over Verdun, France, in 1916.

Bullard was born in Columbus, Georgia, in 1894 to a Martiniquan father and a Creek Indian mother. After fleeing the Ku Klux Klan in his town, Bullard traveled around the country, taking odd jobs before stowing away on a ship to Europe. He worked as a longshoreman in England to support himself, and later became a boxer. Bullard was living in France when World War I broke out, so he enlisted in the French Foreign Legion to fight against the Germans. He saw heavy combat action as a member of the 170th Regiment, known as "the swallows of death" by the Germans. Bullard volunteered for the French Air Service and flew his bi-winged Spad fighter plane on patrols over the city of Verdun in the northeastern part of France.

Bullard became a distinguished fighter pilot. He flew 20 missions against the Germans and was wounded several times while engaging in aerial battles with enemy aircraft (after one encounter, Bullard counted 96 bullet holes in his plane). Yet when America entered the war in the spring of 1917, he was denied a transfer to the U.S. Army Air Corps. American doctors cited his flat feet as the reason; Bullard informed them that those feet had walked all over France while he was in the infantry. Next he was told he had large tonsils; Bullard is said to have replied that he was lucky he wasn't an opera singer. All the American fliers were transferred back home to serve in the Air Corps, but Bullard was not among them. The United States armed services were not integrated, so there was no unit for Bullard to join.

Bullard remained in France, boxing a little while longer before opening a nightclub that boasted such notable guests as Charlie Chaplin, F. Scott Fitzgerald, and Ernest Hemingway. Bullard served his adopted country again shortly before the outbreak of World War II. For French intelligence, he would listen in on conversations among German officers in his club. Eventually he returned to America, and was a frequent invited guest to the French embassy during ceremonial functions. French general Charles de Gaulle presented Bullard with its country's highest award, the Legion of Honor.

Bullard lived out the rest of his life living in a modest room that he rented in Harlem. He was later discovered working as an elevator operator in the National Broadcasting Company (NBC) building by *Today Show* host Dave Garroway. Bullard died of cancer on October 12, 1961, and was buried in his French Legionnaire's uniform. He left behind a detailed memoir of the many fascinating escapades during his lifetime that was later published under the title *The Black Swallow of Death*. In 1992, a bronze bust of Eugene Jacques Bullard was unveiled at the Smithsonian Air and Space Museum in Washington, D.C.

While Bullard was flying patrols over the skies of France, a young black woman living in the United States named Bessie Coleman longed to fly. She wanted to take a plane up high among the clouds and pilot the aircraft into swoops, flips, and spins the way she had seen fighter planes photographed in newspapers accompanying reports on the war in Europe. At a time when women in general faced many restrictions—they didn't have the right to vote until the passage of the Nineteenth Amendment to the United States Constitution in 1920—black women had even fewer opportunities open to them.

Though women lagged behind their male flying counterparts, there were a few pioneers who managed to break through in the early days of aviation. On August 1, 1911, Michigan-born Harriet Quimby became the first American woman to earn her pilot's license. A fiery and independent woman, Quimby was

In 1911, Harriet Quimby became the first American woman to earn a pilot's license. Her achievement paved the way for other female pilots, including black aviator Bessie Coleman.

the quintessential model for today's modern woman. She made her way by carving out a successful career as a photojournalist, was financially independent, and took care of both of her parents.

Even though America's most famous female aviator, Amelia Earhart, didn't take her first flying lesson until 1921 or complete her famous solo transatlantic flight until 1932, she is credited with opening the new field of aviation to women. She was the first person to fly from Hawaii to the United States mainland and was the first person to make solo flights over both the Atlantic and Pacific Oceans. Earhart received a lot of publicity and recognition for her feats in aviation, but at the same time, a young black woman from Atlanta, Texas, was overcoming both gender and racial obstacles to get her chance to fly.

Bessie Coleman, who grew up picking cotton in the fields of Texarkana, Texas, became the first black American to fly in the United States. She was born into a large family (she was the 12th of 13 children) in 1892. Growing up poor and black in the south, Coleman didn't have an easy childhood. Coleman's mother, a former slave, knew the value of an education and instilled its importance in her children. Despite the odds, Bessie Coleman graduated from her one-room school and even attended college for a semester before running out of money. Early on in her life, Coleman learned not to allow the limitations others tried to place on her to deter her from her goals.

When Coleman decided she wanted to become a pilot, she saved money from her job to pay for flying lessons to earn her pilot's license. Unfortunately, she discovered that aviation schools in America were not open to blacks, and no instructors would teach a black person to fly. Coleman had no options until she met *Chicago Defender* publisher Robert Abbott in 1920. Abbott, a staunch civil rights advocate, used his newspaper to denounce the violence and discrimination against black people in America. Abbott knew that Eugene Bullard had learned to fly in France, so he helped Coleman get accepted into the French Fédération Aéronautique Internationale flight school. With Abbott's financial help, Coleman sailed for France in 1921.

After nine months Coleman earned her pilot's license and returned to America, determined to raise money to open her own flight school so other blacks could learn to fly. She decided to perform air shows, entertaining paying crowds below with daredevil moves—flying rolls, loops, and dives, sometimes even climbing out onto the plane's wing while another pilot flew the plane. She gave her first air show at Curtiss Field just outside of New York City, and followed that with a show in Chicago. Coleman's friend Abbott sponsored the shows.

Soon Coleman was traveling around the country performing her air shows while continuing to save the earnings from the ticket sales to open her flying school. Just a few more performances would earn the money she needed to do so. While rehearsing for a show in Jacksonville, Florida, on April 30, 1926, Coleman was unable to pull the plane out of a maneuver. She was thrown out of the cockpit and plunged to her death. Coleman was buried in Chicago, and every year on the anniversary of her death, passing planes drop roses on her grave.

Fortunately, Coleman's death did not bring to an end the dream of opening a flight school for blacks. Black businessman and army veteran William J. Powell had somehow convinced a white flight school in Los Angeles to accept him as a student. He earned his pilot's license and in 1929 founded a flying school and club. In tribute to America's first black female pilot, Powell named it after Bessie Coleman. Powell's own dream was to demonstrate that blacks had the same talents and skills to fly as whites, hoping to dispel some of the prejudicial beliefs against blacks in America.

As Powell and other members of the Coleman Club continued to entertain by performing air shows, Powell also worked behind the scenes to persuade blacks to get involved with the business end of aviation. He published a periodical called *Black Wings* that included articles about other opportunities in the aviation industry, and he encouraged black businessmen to launch new commercial airline carriers, construct new airports, and get into the manufacturing and design of planes and aircraft parts.

While other early aviators both black and white continued

to entertain eager audiences on the ground with their aerial stunt shows and flying maneuvers, serious pilots began to demonstrate the invaluable commercial benefits of the airplane. Planes could be used to transport people and cargo over long distances in shorter time than ground vehicles. Endurance flight was the next test. It was white pilot Charles A. Lindbergh who was the first to succeed in flying nonstop from the United States to Europe, a 3,600-mile journey. Taking off from Roosevelt Field on Long Island, New York, at 7:52 A.M. on May 20, 1927, Lindbergh arrived at Le Bourget Field in Paris, France, 33 hours, 30 minutes, and 29.8 seconds later to a cheering crowd of 150,000 well-wishers. Transatlantic flight was now a reality.

By the end of the 1920s, only 12 of the 18,000 licensed pilots in the United States were black. Despite their lopsided numbers, blacks continued to be a part of the ever-growing advancements in flying. Two of the members of the Bessie Coleman Club, James Herman Banning and Thomas C. Allen, teamed up to try to become the first blacks to fly coast to coast. In 1926, Banning, a native of Oklahoma who had studied engineering at Iowa State College, wanted to learn how to fly. He applied to several flight schools, but was turned down by all of them. Determined, Banning found an army officer in Iowa who agreed to give him lessons. Two years later, Banning joined Powell and his group in Los Angeles.

Thomas Allen, a young black mechanic who had helped Powell set up air shows in Oklahoma, eventually hitchhiked his way to Los Angeles to join the Coleman Club. He and Banning became friends and decided to pair up and take the transcontinental flight together. With a plane purchased by Arthur Dennis, a gambler who went by the nickname "Small Black," and donations from friends to buy enough gasoline to keep them in the air, Banning and Allen left Los Angeles in September 1932. Dubbed "The Flying Hobos," they needed to make several stops to raise money to refuel and make some repairs en route to their final destination of Long Island, New York. The pair took twenty-one days to complete the 3,300-mile journey (they actually made the trip in 42 flight hours) and went into the official history books as the first blacks to successfully fly from coast to coast.

One year after Banning and Allen made their historic flight, businessman C. Alfred "Chief" Anderson and Dr. Albert Forsythe became the first black men to make a round-trip flight. In July 1933, Anderson and Forsythe flew from Atlantic City, New Jersey, to Los Angeles, California. They then headed back to the East Coast, landing in New York City before returning west and bringing the plane down safely in San Francisco, California. The pair also made a successful flight to Canada before taking on a more personal mission in 1934. Taking off from Miami, Florida, in their plane *Booker T. Washington*, Anderson and Forsythe embarked on a journey they named the Pan-American Goodwill Flight. The pair planned to make stops in 21 nations in the Caribbean and South America to demonstrate the skill of black pilots as well as to encourage better relations between blacks and whites. Though their journey ended when the *Booker T. Washington* was damaged in Trinidad, Anderson and Forsythe contributed much to the morale of blacks back home.

As the number of licensed black pilots grew, they also began establishing more flight schools and organizations, as well as getting involved in other aspects of aviation. In 1931, John C. Robinson and Cornelius Coffey founded the Challenger Air Pilot Association in Chicago. Robinson and Coffey, both auto mechanics, met in Detroit, Michigan, in 1925. The two attended the Curtiss-Wright Aeronautical School and earned master mechanics degrees in 1931. After founding Challenger, Robinson and Coffey recruited other black members. Among the first to join were Janet Harmon Bragg, a nurse from Georgia, and Willa Brown, a preacher's daughter from Kentucky.

Stunt pilot Herbert Julian (left) and his assistant, William J. Powell, pose in front of their airplane in 1932. Members of the Challenger Air Pilot Association went on barnstorming tours and held shows at airfields such as the Harlem Airport, thrilling the crowds with spectacular aerial performances.

Eventually, Coffey and Brown wed. The couple, along with Bragg, made the first memorial flight over Bessie Coleman's grave. When Challenger members were refused access to white-owned airstrips, they bought some land in the black community of Robbins, Illinois, and built their own.

In 1933, Coffey and Brown founded the second black flight school. The Coffey School of Aeronautics made its home at the Harlem Airport, in southwest Chicago. That same year black pilots finally had a national organization of their own with the establishment of Negro Airmen International, Inc. Beginning in 1934, members of Challenger went out on barnstorming tours. Many of the air shows were held at the Harlem Airport, where stunt pilots including Willie "Suicide" Jones, Dorothy Darby, Herbert Julian, and Chauncey E. Spencer treated audiences to spectacular performances.

When the Spanish Civil War broke out in 1936, several American pilots went overseas to help fight the takeover by Fascist dictator Francisco Franco. Among the Americans fighting to defeat Franco was black pilot James Peck. Both the Air Corps and the navy had turned down Peck, who received his pilot's license after spending two years at the University of Pittsburgh. In Spain, Peck flew combat missions with pilots from other countries, including Brazil, the Dominican Republic, and Russia. Some accounts credit Peck with shooting down five enemy aircraft, but Peck made no mention of the downings in his books *Armies With Wings* and *So You Want to Fly*, in which he wrote about his wartime experiences.

Despite the courageous efforts of people like Peck, Franco and his Fascists were victorious. At the same time Franco was cementing his hold over Spain, Adolf Hitler's German army was expanding its empire. By 1939, Germany had overrun Czechoslovakia, annexed Austria, and invaded Poland. Recognizing that a second world war loomed over Europe, several countries including the United States were making preparations. The military buildup included making weapons and ammunition, training soldiers, and constructing the ships and planes that would transport the means to conduct a war. The United States government was also instituting a Civilian Pilot Training Program (CPTP) to train college men for the Air Corps.

By the time Germany invaded Poland in September 1939, more than 120 blacks in the United States held pilot's licenses. As the inevitability of a wider-scale war moved closer to America, blacks wanted to sign up for the Air Corps. Unfortunately, many obstacles in the way of that aim would have to be overcome first.

Segregation was a part of black military life even beyond the shores of America. Here, members of the Eighth Army Corps stationed in England stand in a segregated line waiting for their meal rations.

3

Rite of Passage

"You mean to tell me, because of your color you can't get into the U.S. Air Corps?"

—Senator Harry S. Truman asking Federal Workers Union boss
Edgar Brown why blacks couldn't fly in the military

As in every war preceding World War II, the high-ranking members of the United States military tried to keep black enlistment and participation in the armed services to a minimum. This occurred despite the fact that within the historic Emancipation Proclamation of 1862, President Abraham Lincoln guaranteed blacks full and open opportunities in the service: "And I further declare and make known that such persons of suitable condition will be received into the armed service of the United States to garrison forts, positions, stations, and other places, and to man vessels of all sorts in said service." What the document failed to eliminate was the standard military policy of segregating blacks from their white counterparts and relegating them to the more menial tasks in a serviceman's life—such as cleaning, cooking, and working in the mess hall or laundry room.

Blacks had performed very well in military service as far back as the Revolutionary War, receiving praise from superiors and commendations for conduct in battle. Yet when they returned home, many black servicemen were treated badly. Racism continued to pervade many cities and towns across America. Life for many blacks living in cities north and south in America was bleak.

It was no different for those who served or wanted to serve in the military. The military branches of the United States had a policy of segregating blacks from whites. They also attempted to limit the role blacks would have in the service. The reasoning of the military brass was threefold. First, the army felt it reflected the desires of the American people and was not meant to be an instrument for social change. Secondly, it was efficient to use personnel according to their skills and capabilities. Finally, and perhaps the most offensive, was the belief that " . . . the level of intelligence and occupational skill of the Negro population is considerably below that of the white."

An official document on the subject of blacks serving in the military was released by the Army War College in 1925. The report concluded that "the black man was physically unqualified for combat duty; was by nature subservient, mentally inferior, and believed himself to be inferior to the white man; was susceptible to the influence of crowd psychology; could not control himself in the face of danger; and did not have the initiative and resourcefulness of the white man."

In 1931 the National Association for the Advancement of Colored People (NAACP), an organization founded in 1909 whose primary focus has been to protect and enhance the civil rights of blacks and other minorities, sent a letter to the War Department requesting the acceptance of blacks into the Army Air Corps. To justify its position on not accepting applications from blacks, the War Department explained in its response, "The colored man had not been attracted to flying in the same way or to the extent of the white man." In addition, because the department had been inundated with applications from college-trained white men, even many white men had to be turned down.

Twelve years after the War Department released its unfavorable assessment of how poorly blacks would serve in the military, it released another report from a different study. These findings identified the type of personality and characteristics a commander might encounter from a black enlistee: "As an individual the Negro is docile, tractable, lighthearted, care free and good-natured. If unjustly treated, he is likely to become surly and stubborn, though this is usually a temporary phase. He is careless, shiftless, irresponsible and secretive. He resents censure and is best handled with praise and by ridicule. He is unmoral, untruthful and his sense of right doing is relatively inferior." Black men were facing a wall of resistance, based on old stereotyping, blatant racism, and unsubstantiated suppositions.

By the end of the 1930s, another world war seemed inevitable. The United States and its military, though not initially engaged in the conflict, nonetheless began making preparations for the possibility of entering the war. In 1939, Congress passed Public Law 18. By authorizing training of military pilots at civilian colleges and universities, the U.S. government launched one of its largest vocational educational programs in its history—referred to as the Civilian Pilot Training Program (CPTP). "Using the facilities of colleges, universities, and commercial flying schools, the CPTP was designed to provide a pool of civilian pilots for military service in the event of war."

The United States military and the federal government had been under strong pressure by the black press, including *Chicago Defender* editor Enoch Waters and civil rights organizations like the NAACP, to include black educational institutions in the Civilian Pilot Training Program. Two black men, Chauncey Spencer and Dale White, actually took the cause straight to Washington, D.C. With friend Edgar Brown, the head of the Federal Workers Union, Spencer and White made a visit to the Capitol.

While walking along the hallway in the Senate office building, Brown stopped and greeted the senator from Missouri, Harry S. Truman, who asked them, "Are you citizens? Do you pay taxes?" An astonished Truman asked, "You mean to tell me, because of your color you can't get into the U.S. Air Corps?" Brown replied that this was true, at which point Truman assured the three men before him that it wouldn't happen again. Shortly after their impromptu meeting, the Committee on Military Appropriations set aside funds for the creation of the CPTP, which would include black colleges and universities.

The creation of the CPTP was good news for the hundreds of black men across America who wanted to train to fly and serve in the Air Corps. Despite the U.S. military's continued policy of not intermingling black and white personnel, several black schools were eligible for the CPTP program within a few months, including Howard University, Hampton Institute, the Coffey School of Aeronautics, and Tuskegee Institute. The government funded the ground and flight school instruction, while the colleges were responsible for providing the flight instructors, physicals for potential candidates, and transportation to the approved CPTP schools.

The Civilian Pilot Training Program was a milestone for blacks in aviation. For years blacks had been denied military leadership roles and specialized training in the armed services because of the belief that they lacked the abilities to handle combat duty. Despite the years of reservations about the capability of blacks to fly and maintain combat aircraft, the government was finally playing a part in facilitating flight training for blacks as well as sharing in the funding to do so. Just a few years after its creation, approximately 400,000 pilots—2,700 of them black—had successfully completed the program.

Still, many were skeptical about the use of blacks in the Air Corps, and many members of the military brass resisted the idea of blacks in combat roles. General H. H. "Hap" Arnold, commander of the Air Corps, believed the issue of blacks in air

Harry Truman was a Missouri senator when he met with Edgar Brown, Chauncey Spencer, and Dale White to discuss the policy of excluding blacks from the Air Corps. Shortly after the meeting, the U.S. government Committee on Military Appropriations set aside funds to create the Civilian Pilot Training Program (CPTP).

units was moot because it was inconceivable to expect white mechanics to take orders from black pilots, and it would take quite a while to train black ground crews the skills necessary to service an airplane. Marine Corps commander General Thomas Holcomb was even more blunt. He stated that the Marines were a "club" that didn't want blacks. President Franklin Roosevelt was

Like many military leaders of his time, President Franklin Roosevelt did not favor full racial integration in the armed forces, believing that blacks should hold only menial jobs—including mess hall duty, and cooking—or provide musical entertainment for troops. His mind would be changed by an unlikely source—his wife, Eleanor.

little more help. At the time, the navy restricted black enlistees to noncombat, menial duties like cooking, cleanup, and work-crew assignments. His idea of black integration in the navy was to assign a black music band to each ship.

As late as 1940, the War Department tried to defend its policy about the "Black issue." In the fall of that year, Assistant Secretary of War Robert P. Patterson sent a memo to Roosevelt concerning the desegregation issue: " . . . The policy of the War Department is not to intermingle colored and white personnel in the same regimental organizations. This policy has been proven satisfactory over a long period of years and to make changes would produce situations destructive to morale and detrimental to the preparations for national defense."

Many in the black leadership community—including NAACP secretary Walter White and A. Philip Randolph, founder of the Brotherhood of Sleeping Car Porters union—felt that including black colleges and universities in the CPTP was just the first step in integrating blacks into all areas of the armed services. On September 27, 1940, White, Randolph, and Urban League representative T. Arnold Hill met with President Roosevelt, Assistant Secretary of War Robert P. Patterson, and Secretary of the Navy Frank Knox to discuss further inclusion of blacks in the military. White, Randolph, and Hill argued that it was "not enough to train pilots alone, but in addition, navigators, bombardiers, gunners, radiomen, and mechanics must be trained in order to facilitate full Negro participation in the air service." The meeting between the men ended with Roosevelt making no commitments. Ultimately, help for their cause would come from an unlikely source—the president's wife, Eleanor Roosevelt.

Secretary of War Henry Stimson appointed Judge William J. Hastie as a civilian aide to help improve conditions for blacks in the military. Hastie had sound credentials— he was a graduate of Harvard Law School and dean of Howard University Law School.

4

The Tuskegee Experiment

"We were all glad when news of the Tuskegee experiment broke in the papers. At least we black fellows would have a chance to fly. We were young; the politics of the matter didn't register just then. We—I—wanted to fly, even if it was in segregated units!"

—A black veteran recalling the announcement
of the "Tuskegee Experiment"

After the September 27th meeting between Roosevelt, White, Randolph, and Hill, the War Department responded to their request to open up more opportunities for blacks in the military. However, the response left much to be desired. The War Department agreed to allow black men to be admitted to the armed services, but only in numbers equal to their percentage in the civilian population. Members of the black press attacked the decision because they felt that it implied that the new policy had the blessing of White, Randolph, and Hill, which it did not.

While the government and the War Department dragged their feet on the issue of segregation, civilian pilot training at the two black selected educational institutions moved forward. Several eager young black men who dreamed of flying scrambled down to Alabama to enroll in the CPTP at Tuskegee Institute. It had taken Tuskegee some time to acquire its CPTP certification because there wasn't an acceptable airfield within the required ten miles of the CPTP institute location. Tuskegee Institute president Dr. Frederick Douglass Patterson and pilot training director G. L. Washington worked with area politicians to secure the use of a white airstrip for the CPTP until one could be built.

Using materials supplied by the institute, many of the CPTP students worked together to build Kennedy Field. They constructed an airplane hangar, a fuel depot, an office, and restrooms. The entire first CPTP class made it through the primary training program. After completing their flight tests, they all received their private pilot licenses. As a result the institute was awarded Civil Aeronautics Authority (CAA) approval to provide secondary flight instruction. Tuskegee was the only black college to earn that approval.

With the presidential election just a few months away, Roosevelt recognized the importance of attracting the black vote. He knew that he had to address the growing concerns regarding the military's racial policies. He responded by writing a personal letter to White, Randolph, and Hill in which he stated, "You may rest assured that further developments of policy will be forthcoming to insure that Negroes are given fair treatment on a non-discrimination basis."

Roosevelt followed his letter by promoting the black service-man Colonel Benjamin O. Davis Sr. to brigadier general, and instructed Secretary of War Henry Stimson to appoint a black civilian aide. Stimson was not happy about the directive. He wrote in his diary, "The Negroes are taking advantage of this period just before [the] election to try to get everything they can in the way of recognition from the army." In spite of finding the motivation behind the decision objectionable, Stimson appointed William H. Hastie, a Harvard Law School graduate and dean of Howard University Law School. Hastie's job entailed developing methods for improving circumstances for blacks in all areas of military service.

Roosevelt was elected to his third term as president (Congress passed the Twenty-Second Amendment to the Constitution limiting the president to two terms in office in 1951). A month later the Army Air Corps announced a plan to establish an "experiment" by creating an all-black fighter pilot squadron. The Ninety-Ninth Fighter Squadron would consist of about 35 pilots and about 300 ground personnel. White officers, however, would still manage the Ninety-Ninth Fighter Squadron. Since it was an insult for white officers to be assigned over black officers (and there were a few), the War Department came up with a compromise. "Volunteer white noncommissioned officers" would be assigned to supervise and instruct the new cadets indefinitely. However, when a black officer qualified, he would replace white officers in the regiment as well as in any available administrative capacity.

The next step was to determine *where* the black pilots would get their training. Five states were mentioned—California, Illinois, Texas, Michigan, and Alabama. Many black supporters favored Chicago, Illinois. The city already had an established black presence at Harlem Air Field, and the Coffey School of Aeronautics and Glenview School were in or near Chicago.

In the spring of 1941, the Tuskegee CPTP received a surprise visit from First Lady Eleanor Roosevelt. She came out to see firsthand how the CPTP was going and to meet CPTP director Charles "Chief" Anderson. During the course of her visit, Mrs. Roosevelt asked Anderson if blacks could really fly airplanes. Anderson replied that indeed they could, and asked the First Lady if she would like to go up for a ride. Much to the horror of her Secret Service Agent escorts, Mrs. Roosevelt accepted. The Secret Service Agents tried in vain to stop her, even putting in a call to the White House. However, the president reportedly said, "Well, if Eleanor wants to fly, she's going to fly."

Chief Anderson took Mrs. Roosevelt up in his Piper J-3 Cub and flew around for about 30 minutes, giving the First Lady an aerial view of the campus and some nearby communities before landing the plane and its important passenger safely on Moton Field, the grassy airstrip near the institute. Mrs. Roosevelt told Chief Anderson, "Well, I guess Negroes can fly," and she thanked him for the ride. When she returned to Washington most believe she told her husband how well "those boys down there" had done. Not long after Mrs. Roosevelt's famous visit, the army announced that the training location for its "experiment" would be Tuskegee Institute.

Many in the black community were stunned by the choice of Tuskegee, Alabama. The south was well known for its racial intolerance. Hate groups like the white-hooded Ku Klux Klan freely committed random acts of violence against blacks, carrying out lynchings and inflicting beatings on men, women, and children with little concern for intervention by law enforcement. There were those, however, who thought the selection of Tuskegee was a fitting tribute to one of their own—prominent black leader and educator Booker T. Washington. A former slave, Washington had built Tuskegee Institute (later renamed Tuskegee University) in 1881.

Though not happy about the decision to form a segregated unit, the NAACP felt that it was at least a step in the right direction. The official announcement of the formation of the all-black fighter squadron came during a press conference on January 16, 1941. The official report stated, "Concurrently, 35 black candidates would be chosen under the Civil Aeronautics Authority from the Civilian Pilot Training Program established by Congress in 1939 to train civilians while they were going to college, and given 30 weeks of flight training under white instructors."

For 15 weeks the cadets would begin their primary training at the institute. After completing the first phase of instruction, the cadets would move on to combat pilot training at the Tuskegee Army Air Field, which had yet to be constructed. While the

During a visit to Tuskegee Institute, First Lady Eleanor Roosevelt asked CPTP director Charles "Chief" Anderson whether blacks could really fly planes. Anderson responded by taking Mrs. Roosevelt on a flight. Back in Washington, she related the story to her husband. Shortly after, Tuskegee was chosen for the army's "experiment."

pilots trained in Alabama, support personnel trained at the Air Corps Technical School at Chanute Field in Illinois. Upon completion of their training, they would be transferred to Tuskegee to join the pilots.

While primary training was being conducted, the Tuskegee

Before Tuskegee Institute could serve as a training facility for pilots and support personnel, it needed additional buildings. Workers built hangers, repair shops, dining halls, and various other structures within six months at a cost of $1.1 million.

Army Air Field (TAAF) would be constructed. The U.S. government decided to award the contract to McKissack and McKissack, Inc., a black architectural and construction company based in Nashville, Tennessee. It was quite an undertaking. Company owners Calvin and Moses McKissack not only had to construct the airplane runways, but the airfield complex also required hangars for the planes, repair shops, dining halls, an infirmary, firehouse, labs, classrooms, barracks, and an administration building. The TAAF project cost the government $1.1 million and was completed in less than six months.

With the official announcement of the location for training the first all-black fighter pilot squadron, a number of things were finally put into motion. The Army Air Corps sent out orders to the personnel who would be transferred to Tuskegee. The corps had to process the massive numbers of applications sent in by black candidates eager to be chosen for the first class of cadets. After years of seeking the right to train and fly as pilots serving in the armed forces, the opportunity for black men across America had finally been achieved. Still, the stipulation that it be a segregated unit left many black leaders and citizens unsatisfied. William Hastie was bold enough to ask the question many were thinking, "How could a black man be expected to fight and defend a country that didn't respect his rights as a citizen?"

Brig. Gen. Benjamin O. Davis Sr. (seated) with his son, Lt. Col. Benjamin O. Davis Jr. The senior Davis was the first black brigadier general in America, and was proud that his son chose to follow in his footsteps. To become a pilot, Davis Jr. had to overcome his own racial hurdles.

5

Earning
Their Wings

*"The eyes of your country and the eyes of your people are upon you.
The success of the venture depends upon you."*

—Major General Walter Weaver to the
first class of trainees, July 19, 1941

espite the official report stating that 35 black pilot trainee
candidates would be chosen for the first class, only 12 cadets
and one officer-in-training made up the class known as 42-C. The
first student chosen was Lieutenant Benjamin O. Davis Jr., the son of
newly promoted Brigadier General Benjamin O. Davis Sr. Young
Lieutenant Davis was the only officer in 42-C. His father was a
lifelong soldier who served in the Spanish-American War in 1898.
Rejected by West Point, Davis Sr. enlisted in the army and served with
the all-black Eighth Infantry. After working his way up through the
ranks to become a first lieutenant, Davis Sr. was left with few options
after combat. Since there were no integrated units in the military, he

was left to teach military science as a Reserve Officers' Training Corps (ROTC) instructor at all-black colleges, including Wilberforce College and Tuskegee Institute.

Though proud that his son wanted to follow him in the service, Davis Sr. was also concerned because he was all too familiar with the racism that pervaded the military. The odds were against his son from even graduating from West Point, as no black man had yet to accomplish that challenge in the twentieth century. Still, after overcoming several hurdles in his path, Benjamin O. Davis Jr. entered West Point Military Academy on July 1, 1932. His life at West Point was dismal and unpleasant—he had no roommate, was "silenced" (which meant none of his classmates would speak to him), and spent four years virtually alone. The ill treatment he endured, however, only gave Davis greater resolve to succeed. He graduated 35th in his class of 236. He applied to the Army Air Corps but was turned down, so after marrying Agatha Scott in the West Point chapel, Davis served at a few military outposts before being assigned to teach military science at Tuskegee Institute.

Having spent several years at Tuskegee, Davis was well aware of the racial problems blacks faced in Alabama and the rest of the south. Years after Tuskegee was chosen for the all-black fighter pilot training "experiment," Davis wrote, "The Air Corps well understood the political mine fields that stood in the way of the airfield's development: the attitude of white citizens of Tuskegee; the attitude of the white officers and enlisted men assigned to the base; the War Department's segregation policies; and the basic question posed by the . . . [Tuskegee] 'experiment.'" Still, for the young black officer who counted among his heroes aviator Charles Lindbergh and had taken his first ride in an airplane after his father paid a barnstormer five dollars, Davis welcomed his selection into the class of 42-C.

Among the other twelve trainees were several college graduates, CPTP participants, a policeman, a factory inspector, and a scholar-athlete. They came from large cities and small towns in

America. The cadet trainees assembled on the grass near the statue of Booker T. Washington on the Tuskegee Institute campus on July 19, 1941, for the initiation ceremony of class 42-C. Dressed in freshly pressed khaki uniforms (except for Lemuel Custis, who had only arrived that morning and had no time to change into a uniform), the cadets listened as Major General Walter Weaver, commander of the United States Army's Southeastern Air Corps Training Command, officiated over the dedication ceremonies. Several members of the military sat in attendance. Others like Army Chief of Staff General George Marshall and Air Corps Chief General Henry "Hap" Arnold sent congratulatory telegrams.

Cadet Custis, who had already made history of sorts by becoming the first black police officer in the state of Connecticut, shared his feelings about that day: "We were enthused because we felt that at last we had a great opportunity in the Air Corps. We were happy to be there. It was a proud feeling. We were focused on the task—didn't feel like pioneers or anything. Later, looking back, we realized our trail breaking role." As for flying, Custis added, "I was consumed with making it, not washing out. Next to my wife, flying has been the greatest love of my life."

The second cadet chosen for the first class, George "Spanky" Roberts, grew up in the small town of Fairmont, West Virginia. A mix of Indian, black, Caucasian, and "a little" Jewish, Roberts was smitten with flying as a teenager. His parents managed to scrape up enough money to take a ride in a four-seater plane. When the pilot offered to let Roberts fly it, he jumped at the chance. For about 20 minutes Roberts piloted the aircraft (despite having to stand to reach the floor petals) and fell in love with aviation. He went on to attend West Virginia State College, where he studied engineering and some psychology. Flying, however, was never far from his thoughts and he "haunted the hell out of the Air Corps" to accept him as a trainee. When the War Department announced the creation of the all-black flight program, Roberts was one of the first contacted.

Capt. Lemuel Custis (left, with Capt. Charles B. Hall) was no stranger to challenges. He had already become the first black police officer in Connecticut before joining the first group of Tuskegee hopefuls as a member of class 42-C.

Two of the cadet trainees accepted were graduates of the CPTP. Charles DeBow grew up in Indiana and attended Hampton Institute, a black educational establishment founded in 1868 in Hampton, Virginia. Mac Ross, another graduate from West Virginia State, wound up being the first Tuskegee flight cadet to survive the crash of a military aircraft. He was able to bail out of the badly smoking plane in time to walk away relatively unharmed. Less concerned for his own safety, Ross worried that his loss of the "several thousand dollar" airplane might wash him out, or worse, put a mark on the entire program. "Maybe they'll think we're incompetent," said Ross. His fears were alleviated when the ensuing investigation determined that the plane crash was not due to anything Ross had done wrong, and he was cleared of any pilot error.

The dedication ceremony was an important event in black aviation history. As excited as the cadet trainees were, however, there were others who remained skeptical. General Weaver was quoted as saying privately to his airmen training officer not to worry about maintaining standards for the new recruits. He just wanted to keep the men happy.

Once the pleasantries were completed, the cadets were given their first reminder of the difficulties that lay ahead. All the commanding officers assigned by the Air Corps were white. The first, Major James Ellison, was a strong advocate of blacks being allowed in the Air Corps. A "by-the-book" commander, Ellison earned the nickname "Straight Arrow." He was quoted on record as saying that he wanted the "Tuskegee Experiment" project to succeed, and his goal was "to fly across the country with a Negro squadron and prove to the nation that it could happen." A sincere and dedicated officer, Ellison could also be blunt. He told the men of 42-C, "Take a good look at the man on your left and on your right, because on graduation day they won't be there."

The cadets privately promised each other that they would all hang in there no matter what happened. They began the primary phase of training in the classroom, studying basic science and engineering subjects they would need to learn to become pilots. The man in charge of supervising the primary instruction was Captain Noel Parrish, who had been a CPTP instructor in Chicago. Parrish showed no signs of racism or skepticism about the "experiment." In time he came to despise the racial segregation mandated by the War Department, and as a training officer soon tired of the silly questions asked of him by prying whites like, "How do Negroes fly?" "Are blacks better fliers because they're closer to nature?" and "Are those really Negroes up there or are you doing it for them?"

Legendary flier Chief Anderson was put in charge of the primary flight training. Here, the cadets would be taught how to maneuver and control an aircraft through the use of controls and foot pedals. Anderson recruited additional staff, hiring both black and white civilian instructors. Some of the black instructors were former CPTP graduates, including Bill Campbell, James T. Wiley, Daniel "Chappie" James, and George "Bill" Terry. The men directly responsible for training the cadets of the Ninety-Ninth were Captain Gabe C. Hawkins, director of basic training; Captain Robert M. Long, director of advanced training; and Major Donald G. McPherson. They were tough on their trainees, sometimes even short-tempered with them, but the cadets recognized and appreciated their experience and skill.

Of the white instructors, the Tuskegee Airmen praised their counterparts. The majority agreed that they were fair, conscientious, and displayed no signs of racism, voluntarily choosing to be at Tuskegee. Wiley went further, explaining, "You have to give them a lot of credit. I don't know if I'd have done it—give up a chance for a career and a chance to make general, as some of them did, in order to train blacks."

Tuskegee offered the cadets little in terms of creature comforts. Until construction of the Tuskegee Army Air Field was completed, the men lived amid pretty dreadful conditions. They lived in tents, ate in a mess hall that was made up of four walls and a dirt floor, and dined in a small area using empty crates for chairs.

Training at Tuskegee included course work in navigation and engineering, as well as in basic science.

What little free time the cadets had was rarely spent away from the base. Downtown Tuskegee, Alabama, was located six miles from the institute, and it was not a welcoming place for blacks. The town employed strict segregation and openly discriminated against blacks, making it difficult to run errands or buy merchandise. The restaurants and the town movie theater had designated areas for black customers. Housing for black civilian instructors was virtually nonexistent.

The townspeople themselves were rather hostile to their new black neighbors, and Tuskegee's town sheriff, Pat Evans, harassed the men at every opportunity. When the townspeople learned of the army's intention to build an airfield to train blacks, they strongly opposed it. Petitions were signed and passed around town; Alabama's senators were inundated with letters. When none of that helped, the citizens of Tuskegee argued that the base would inhibit any expansion of the town. Once it was pointed out that the base was going to be several miles away, the movement to block the base's construction ended. Even with the issue dropped, the black cadets and support personnel knew they would not be welcome in town, so most of them avoided going off the base.

The cadets faced other pressures too. Graduating classes were limited by the War Department's quota to a maximum of ten pilots each, and the maximum number of pilots per year was kept to 52, no matter how well one performed. Those restrictions alone meant many qualified black men would be excluded from participation in the "experiment," and the chances that one would earn your wings were minute. The cadets knew they had to "stay the course" if the "experiment" was to succeed, and they channeled their energies into their studies rather than be distracted by issues beyond their control.

Besides classroom instruction, the cadets began learning the workings of the airplanes and how to fly them. Flying lessons began at Moton Field in August. By then some of the 13 recruits had "washed out," a term used when a pilot candidate failed at any stage of the training program. Moving to the airfield from the classroom where the cadets had studied math, aviation map reading, navigation, communications, brought the remaining cadets one step closer to earning their pilot's wings.

The first trainer plane was a PT-17, a biplane without retractable landing gear. A flight instructor flew with the trainee, working the controls and demonstrating the plane's various maneuvering capabilities. The cadets learned how to change the plane's speed, altitude, and direction by using "the stick," or by manipulating the control

Pilot trainees at Tuskegee learned to fly in various aircraft including the P-40, shown here. Besides basic maneuvers, the pilots also had to learn to fly in formation and engage in aerial battles with the enemy.

column and foot pedals to move panels positioned on the plane's wings and tail. They learned how to take off, land, and how to handle emergency situations like engine failure. The cadets were expected to follow their instructor's commands exactly. Any deviation was immediate grounds for "washing out."

After receiving eight hours of flight training with an instructor, the cadet was expected to take the plane up on his own. Those who made it to the solo flight stage recognized the significance of that moment. In recalling his first solo flight, Cadet Lemuel Custis said, "Soloing was a good feeling. I knew it was only the first tiny step in the journey toward getting those wings. But it was a big deal."

Only five cadets—Benjamin O. Davis Jr., George "Spanky" Roberts, Mac Ross, Charles DeBow, and Lemuel Custis—moved on to basic training at Tuskegee Army Air Field. There the cadets learned how to fly bigger planes including the BT-13, the AT-6, and finally the P-40 fighter plane. The BT-13 allowed the cadets to practice landings, spins, inverted flying, loops, vertical climbs, and other maneuvers in a larger plane. Davis particularly enjoyed a maneuver called *chandelles,* which he described as "abrupt, steep, climbing turns that had to be smoothly executed to gain maximum altitude and change of direction at the expense of airspeed." Few were surprised when Davis became the first black man to officially solo an aircraft as an officer of the Army Air Corps on September 2, 1941.

After mastering the BT-13s, the cadets moved on to the AT-6 with their 650-horsepower engines. Cruising at 160 miles an hour, the AT-6 demanded much faster reflexes from the cadets than the BT-13s. It was while learning how to fly the AT-6s that the pilot trainees were introduced to flying in formation. The AT-6 was also the first airplane the cadets flew that had retractable landing gear, so it was one more element in their flight training to learn.

On December 7, 1941, while Davis, Roberts, Ross, DeBow, and Custis were busy learning how to fly the P-40 fighter planes that would bring them nearer to the end of their training, the Japanese bombed the United States naval base at Pearl Harbor in Hawaii. The sneak attack led the United States to declare war on Japan, thrusting them into World War II, a conflict that had already been raging for two years and on two fronts—Europe and the Pacific.

Other black pilot cadet classes were in various stages of their own training at the time of the attack on Pearl Harbor. On March 7, 1942, the five-member Class 42-C, having mastered the skills necessary of a fighter pilot, completed their training. Davis, Roberts, Ross, DeBow, and Custis had earned their wings and in the process demonstrated that the black pilot program had succeeded.

At graduation, each man stood proudly as his wife or mother was given the honor of pinning the silver flying wings onto his uniform. Lemuel Custis, George Roberts, Mac Ross, and Charles DeBow were promoted to the rank of second lieutenant in the newly named Army Air Force. Davis was promoted to captain. Army chief of air staff General George Stratemeyer expressed what everyone was thinking when he said to the class, "The vast unseen audience of your well-wishers senses that this graduation is an historic moment. . . . Future graduates of this school will look up to you as Old Pilots. They will be influenced profoundly by the examples you set." The men of class 42-C had achieved the impossible. They proved that black men could learn to fly and pilot military aircraft. Now that America was at war, they were eager to prove themselves in combat.

Tuskegee cadets learned how to send and receive code. Many black Americans rushed to enlist after the December 1941 attack on Pearl Harbor, but the army was still keeping rigid quotas at Tuskegee. Training class size was limited to ten students.

6

The Ninety-Ninth Prepares for War

"As we said our goodbyes, we pushed far back and away the ugliness that we had endured. After all, we had successfully passed the first obstacle standing in the way of a better life for all of us—learning how to fly airplanes."

—Ninety-Ninth Squadron troop commander
Benjamin O. Davis Jr.

One day after receiving his wings, Charles DeBow was walking down a street in Montgomery, Alabama. A local white resident stopped him to ask why blacks wanted to fly. After thinking about the question for a few days, DeBow wrote down his answer and submitted it in an article in *The American Magazine*. DeBow's answer was three-fold: he flew for his parents, who had worked hard to give their son an opportunity to be anything he believed he could be; he flew for his race; and he flew for his country. Despite its flaws, America was the land of opportunity, and it offered much more freedom than Nazism.

Segregation against blacks in America was the greatest contradiction to the three major documents—the Declaration of Independence, the Constitution, and the Bill of Rights—on which the United States was founded. Yet when America's freedom and safety were threatened, blacks did not hesitate to step up to help defend her. After the Japanese attack on Pearl Harbor, black men headed to military recruiting offices in greater numbers than anyone had anticipated. Many applied for admission to the Army Air Corps, but the army kept to its rigid quotas at Tuskegee, permitting only ten students at a time to go through training. Because of the army's myopic vision, many good candidates were either refused acceptance into the pilot training program, or had to wait several months in the hopes of being called up.

Away from the bureaucratic issues within the military, the men training to fly at Tuskegee and the aviation support personnel training concurrently—first at Chanute Field Technical School and then Maxwell Air Force Base in Montgomery—were doing well. One trainee, Harry Sheppard, was studying electrical engineering at City College of New York when his cousin Walt told him about the Air Corps opening up a program for blacks. Walt suggested enthusiastically that they apply for the aviation technical support crews. Sheppard was ambivalent about the idea. Ironically, after taking a preliminary test that covered subjects including history, math, economics, and current events, Walt failed and Sheppard passed.

Sheppard was inducted as a private and joined more than 200 other trainees who would get instruction to fill positions as communications technicians, hydraulic specialists, electrical specialists, and engine mechanics. The schedule was grueling— classes began at 6:30 A.M. and ended at 2:30 in the afternoon. Though they attended an integrated school, the black trainees were segregated from the other students just like the pilot trainees had been. Again, these men came from all walks of life. There were college students, college graduates, even professionals who wanted a chance to be a part of the Air Corps. Sheppard and the members of his class left Chanute in the late fall of 1941 with the distinction of having the highest grade point average of any class that had passed through the doors of the school.

While the pilot cadets and technical trainees worked hard to overcome the racial barriers and attitudes that confronted them every day, they were still subjected to the bias and ignorance of those around them. When Sheppard's group was transferred to Maxwell Field, they were relegated to menial tasks like guard duty and sweeping the streets instead of allowing them to do the work they had trained for.

William Hastie had not only been concerned about the success of the "Tuskegee Experiment" but also about possible racial tensions between the black trainees and the white officers as well as from the townspeople. His concerns were well founded. Besides bigoted sheriff Pat Evans, new TAAF base commander Colonel Frederick von Kimble had his own racial agenda. His presence did not contribute a positive atmosphere to the base. He strictly enforced segregation and did not provide the leadership and support the cadets expected. He ordered signs posted designating "Colored" and "White" rest-rooms, water fountains, and other places on the base so the cadets knew where they could and could not go. Many of the recruits felt demoralized by von Kimble's restrictive, racist command style.

Fortunately before he could do much damage, von Kimble was replaced at TAAF. Colonel Parrish was named base com-mander and began smoothing things over with the men. He ordered all the segregation signs removed, joined the Black Officers' Club (often dining there), and listened supportively as the men vented their anger and frustration until the tensions eased. Lieutenant DeBow expressed the feelings most of the black pilots and trainees had: "We didn't want people to love

In an effort to boost morale, the base commander at Tuskegee, Colonel Noel Parrish, brought celebrities to the institute. Here, Lena Horne is shown with some of the pilots at Tuskegee. Other celebrities who passed through include comedian Eddie "Rochester" Anderson and boxing champion Joe Louis.

us or give us any special privileges. We wanted to be respected for being first rate pilots in the Army Air Corps. Nothing more. Nothing less."

Parrish went one step further. He knew living conditions were difficult for the men, who were away from home, isolated on a base with few comforts, and afraid to go into town. There was little diversion from the day-to-day training. With the help of Dr. Patterson, Parrish brought entertainers like singer Lena Horne, comedian Eddie "Rochester" Anderson, and heavyweight boxing champ Joe Louis onto the base to visit with the troops. It was just one way Parrish tried to boost morale and show his men the respect they deserved.

With America now at war, there was a greater urgency to train personnel for combat. The Ninety-Ninth Fighter Squadron was the first activated by the Air Corps. Three squadrons formed a group, but the Ninety-Ninth had yet to receive a group assignment. More fliers were needed to create a second squadron. They would come from additional pilot training classes that followed closely behind 42-C. Classes 42-D and 42-E were scheduled to graduate in five-week intervals. In preparation for the next squadron activation, the Air Corps appointed one of the first five to graduate from the program, Second Lieutenant Mac Ross, to command the 100th Fighter Squadron.

Ten cadets were enrolled in class 42-D in August 1941. Unfortunately only three—Charles Dryden, Clarence Jamison, and Sidney Brooks—graduated. Dryden had been waiting for his moment to fly since childhood. As a baby he used to throw pieces of paper up in the air saying, "Airplane, airplane." As an adolescent, his interest in aviation continued. He read whatever he could get his hands on that relayed stories about the flying aces of World War I. Dryden was attending Community College of New York and studying mechanical engineering when he decided to enroll in the CPTP. Because of his training in the CPTP program, Dryden excelled in the classroom courses like meteorology and navigation. On receiving his pilot's wings, Dryden said, "The highlight of my entire life, even up to now was receiving my wings. I've never had such euphoria before or since as I did that day."

Clarence Jamison, a native of Cleveland, actually knew the Davis family before he came to Tuskegee. While a student at

Wilberforce University, Jamison joined the ROTC and was taught by Benjamin O. Davis Sr. He transferred to the University of Chicago and enrolled in the CPTP to earn extra credit. As soon as the United States entered the war, Jamison wrote a letter to First Lady Eleanor Roosevelt expressing his desire to join the Air Corps. Not long after he sent the letter, he heard from the War Department and soon after was accepted into the Tuskegee pilot program. The last of the trio, Sidney Brooks, was a very athletic member of the Ninety-Ninth. He was big on football and basketball, and took the younger cadets under his wing, acting like a "big brother."

The third class, 42-E, began its training in September. Only four cadets—Lee Rayford, Sherman White, George Knox, and Bernard Knighten—completed training and earned their wings. Knighten, like many of the cadet trainees, had a college degree but had never even flown in an airplane. He graduated as a social science major from Dillard University, but could only get a job as a Pullman train car waiter working the Chicago–Los Angeles route. After he heard about the Air Corps program at Tuskegee, he took the exam. He had also applied to law school and divinity school. When he returned from one of his train runs, there were three letters of acceptance waiting in his mail, but Knighten chose the aviation program.

Knighten roomed with Sherman White, the most uncoordinated man he had ever met. White couldn't even keep the cadence during marching drills. White, who had been Clarence Jamison's best friend at the University of Chicago, learned to fly before he could drive an automobile. One of his strongest assets, and one that was especially helpful while in the pilot's program, was his easygoing personality. Knox was a quiet man, but a good cadet trainee. Lee Rayford was the most popular cadet with the ladies. Handsome and charming, Rayford was the man who was the life of every party and didn't look the part of a soldier, but became an excellent pilot.

Out of the first three classes, only 12 cadets out of 30 earned their wings. To some it seemed that the air force was offering very little encouragement to ensure the success of the program. Concerned about the high number of "washouts," Colonel Parrish pushed for the fourth class to be formed from CPTP graduates. His intuition about a greater success rate paid off. Of the 28 trainees who started the class, 14 completed the program and graduated in June 1942. Two of the graduates were former CPTP instructors Bill Campbell and James Wiley. Others included Charlie Hall, a student of Wiley's at the CPTP; Erwin Lawrence; Spann Watson; Lou Purnell; and Faythe McGinnis. Sadly, McGinnis never made it into combat. While on a flight as part of an eight-plane formation, McGinnis's plane never came out of a loop maneuver. He was the first Tuskegee officer to die.

While the Ninety-Ninth awaited orders for combat, more aviation support personnel arrived at TAAF. Among the new enlistment specialists was Bessie Coleman's nephew, Arthur Freedman. Many of the pilots believed Bessie would have been proud to know that her nephew was also a part of black aviation history. It was particularly poignant because Freedman, like so many before him, had come up against such strong resistance from the military and the white community.

As the summer dragged on, no word came from the high command as to when the Ninety-Ninth Fighter Squadron was going to receive combat orders. With the fourth class earning their wings, the Ninety-Ninth now had the full complement of pilots needed to fill out the squadron. The 35 enlisted men who joined the pilots in the Ninety-Ninth had defied all predictions. Training to service the planes at Chanute Field took only nine months to a year—while Air Corps commander General H. H. "Hap" Arnold originally predicted that it would take nine *years* to train black ground personnel.

While awaiting their orders, the members of the Ninety-Ninth continued to practice their fighter skills flying in P-40s, the planes known as "Flying Tigers." Sometimes nicknamed the "Flying Coffin," the P-40 was the plane the pilots would fly in actual combat. Continuing practice flying in the P-40 was encouraged, as it was a difficult aircraft to handle. A later pilot cadet graduate, Alexander Jefferson, said the P-40 "had a bad habit of pulling to the left as you were going down the runway for a takeoff." Custis remembered some advice he was given when he started training on the P-40: "Fly the airplane, don't let it fly you." The P-40 aircraft was a good plane, but it had its limitations. It couldn't outclimb the Germans' fighter planes of choice, the Messerschmidt 109 or the Focke-Wulf 190. The P-40 also didn't have the speed or altitude capabilities of the German aircraft. However, it could take a lot of punishment.

Having to sit out the wait for their combat orders to come through, the men of the Ninety-Ninth continued to train and stay in shape for the task ahead. New recruits watched as the Ninety-Ninth marched at 120 steps a minute down the streets of the base, all the while chanting their fight song:

Fight! Fight! Fight! Fight—Fight—Fight!
The fighting Ninety-Ninth!
We are the heroes of the night.
To hell with Axis might!
Rat-tat! Rat-tat-tat!
Round in planes we go
When we fly, Ninety-Ninth
This is how we go.

The pilots practiced their flight maneuvers, night flying, and target-hitting skills. Many of the men became so proficient at nailing gunnery targets that the top brass banned them from flying during certain hours so there would be targets left for other pilot trainees. Sometimes boredom would overtake

It wasn't until 1943 that the Ninety-Ninth was finally called to combat. They flew the P-40s (shown here) on which they had trained, earning both honor for their country and respect for themselves.

them and they attempted dangerous maneuvers. Situated near Tuskegee was a lake that had two bridges and a power line that were about 20 feet off the ground. To amuse themselves, some of the pilots would fly under the bridges and under the power line before flying into a loop, and then do it all over again. Perhaps they didn't sense the danger, or perhaps they didn't think anything bad would happen—but eventually, tragedy struck. Pilots Walter Lawson and Richard Dawson took out an AT-6. While attempting the bridge-wire stunt, Lawson didn't pull through. Dawson was killed, and Lawson was later found wandering in a dazed state in the woods nearby.

While the pilots trained by participating in mock aerial dog-fights against one another, the ground personnel were honing their own skills. They managed to change plane engines in one-third the time it normally took to execute the job. Some pilots practiced formation flying, leading to their being awarded Air Corps commendations for precision flying. It looked like orders might be forthcoming when Davis was promoted to lieutenant colonel, taking command of the Ninety-Ninth Fighter Squadron on August 24, 1942, just five months after earning his wings. It was becoming a habit for Davis to be involved in some sort of history-making event. On this occasion Davis was taking command of the first black squadron in United States history. Still, no orders came.

The Ninety-Ninth waited through the rest of 1942. While they waited for their opportunity to perform in combat, the army was preparing two black infantry divisions, the Ninety-Second and the Ninety-Third. In general, treatment of blacks in the service hadn't improved despite the success of the Ninety-Ninth black pilots. The Ninety-Second were training at Fort Huachuca in Arizona, one of the most desolate army posts in the United States. The Ninety-Third infantrymen were sent to the Pacific theater, but they were not put into combat. Instead they were divided up among white units and used as laborers, truck drivers, and security guards.

One black cavalry unit that was actually dispatched to North Africa was divided up among other battalions to be used for labor work. It was black soldiers who built the Burma Road to China and the Alcan Highway in Alaska. Black nurses were subjected to segregation too. Because they didn't have wounded black soldiers to take care of, they were relegated to caring for German prisoners of war. There were 4,000 black women in the Women's Army Corps (WAC), but while the white WACs were given secretarial desk jobs, the black WACs did domestic work, being assigned laundry and mess hall duty.

The men of the Ninety-Ninth were itching to get into combat. They had much to prove to the military and the white populace back home. They were a confident bunch and recognized the enormity of their opportunity to demonstrate that blacks were as able and capable as anyone. Though the Ninety-Ninth was ready to go at a moment's notice, the War Department wasn't ready to send them into combat. Part of the problem with receiving combat orders had to do with the army making a decision about where to deploy the Ninety-Ninth. At first the Air Corps wanted to send the Ninety-Ninth to Liberia to fight the Germans, who had taken control of North Africa. But by the end of 1942, the Allied forces had succeeded in pushing the Germans back toward the Mediterranean Sea. Again the question became: where to send the Ninety-Ninth Fighter Squadron?

While the War Department was trying to decide where to send the Ninety-Ninth, some people were wondering if they intended to send them at all. Nearly seven months had passed since the last squadron had completed their training, and people in the black community as well as in Washington began to ask why the Ninety-Ninth had not been sent into combat. William Hastie, fed up with the Air Corps' inaction, resigned his position as civilian aide to Secretary of War Henry Stimson. A few weeks later Hastie wrote a scathing pamphlet that he titled *On Clipped Wings*. Within its pages, Hastie vented all the feelings he had about the military's resistance to allowing blacks to serve in the Air Corps: "By not wanting the Negro in the first place and by doubting its capacity, the Air Command has committed itself psychologically to . . . actions which become major obstacles to the success of Negroes in the Air Force."

Even Eleanor Roosevelt questioned the Air Corps about why the Ninety-Ninth was not being put into combat service. Amid the building pressure, Secretary of War Stimson made a visit to the TAAF. He inspected the Ninety-Ninth troops and visited extensively with Colonel Parrish. He returned to Washington quite impressed by what he had seen and heard. The man who just a few years ago was certain that blacks could never learn to become pilots commended the Ninety-Ninth by stating they were "outstanding by any standard."

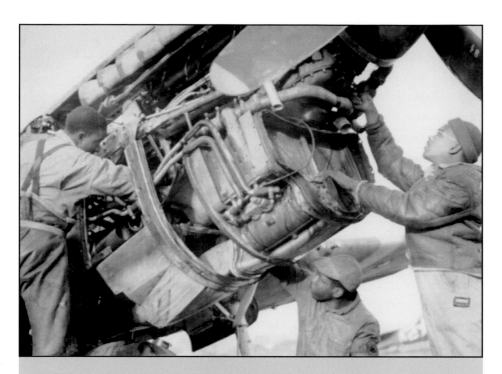

While the Ninety-Ninth awaited orders to fly into combat, ground personnel stayed busy. With practice they became capable of changing plane engines in one-third the time it usually took.

It didn't take long after Stimson's visit for things to get busy at the institute. Training and flight practice were accelerated. Pilots were training on a new technological tool—radar—which allowed them to track other aircraft and bring them back to a landing area safely. On March 25, the men of the Ninety-Ninth squadron took their last non-combat flights. Earl King's plane collided with the infamous power line over the lake, and King was killed. Jim McCullin, a cadet from the sixth class, quickly replaced him.

On April 1, 1943, the men of the Ninety-Ninth finally heard the two words they had been waiting over a year to hear— "Move out." Colonel Parrish, one of the strongest supporters of the Tuskegee program and the men who formed the Ninety-Ninth met with all of them to say good-bye, saying, "You are fighting men now. You have made the team. Your future is now being handed into your own hands. Your future, good or bad, will depend largely on how determined you are not to give satisfaction to those who would like to see you fail."

The following morning, the proud men of the Ninety-Ninth boarded a train that would take them to New York. From there, they would head to North Africa, and into the combat they had trained so hard to join.

Members of the Ninety-Ninth, shown here near Fez, were elated to be called to combat. Despite initial fears, they found that members of the Twenty-Seventh Fighter Group, all of whom were white, did not take the army's segregation rule to heart.

7

Fighting for Country, Fighting for Respect

"A pilot or a man of whatever color is just as good as he proves himself to be. Our pilots had pretty good alibis for being failures if they wanted to use them. When the test came, they had to fight just as men, Americans against a common enemy."

—Noel Parrish, Commander,
Tuskegee Army Air Force Base

On April 15, 1943, the men of the Ninety-Ninth boarded the *S.S. Mariposa,* a converted luxury liner now painted the dull gray color of military ships. Four hundred members of the Ninety-Ninth and 3,500 white servicemen fell under the command of Lieutenant Colonel Benjamin O. Davis Jr. It was the first time a black officer had ever commanded white troops. Davis was very honored to have this command, feeling that he and his men were now an integral part of the military war effort.

As the *Mariposa* sailed out of New York harbor, Davis expected that he and his men were leaving behind all the racial discrimination and injustices they had endured to make it this far. Much to their disappointment, on just their first day at sea, the black troops were greeted on deck by a rope that separated them from the white servicemen. Pilot Lou Purnell expressed what everyone was thinking, " . . . it didn't worry us. We were on our way to defend our country. We were flying. We had done the impossible."

The *Mariposa* brought the troops to Casablanca, the exotic city on the Atlantic coast of Morocco on April 24th. From there the troops traveled by truck to Oued N'ja, their training base located just outside of Fez. While awaiting further orders, the pilots trained on the P-40L, a new War Hawk fighter plane that could reach speeds of up to 350 miles per hour and could climb more than 20,000 feet.

Much to their delight, the Ninety-Ninth received a warm reception from the men of the all-white Twenty-Seventh Fighter Group. Despite the military's segregation policies, the Twenty-Seventh chose to ignore them. The pilots from both groups trained together many times while they awaited their next orders. The pilots of the Ninety-Ninth were also the recipients of another surprise—a visit by "Flying Tiger" veteran flier Lieutenant Colonel Philip Cochran. He trained with the Ninety-Ninth squadron pilots and taught them some important aerial combat maneuvers he had learned from his own fighting missions. He was with them constantly for a week—dining, sleeping, flying, and talking with the men as if he was part of the squadron. Cochran developed a special bond with the men and he had a tremendous effect on them. One pilot summarized what Cochran's time with them had meant, saying that "He imbued all of us with some of his own very remarkable fighting spirit."

After spending a month in Fez, the Ninety-Ninth joined the Thirty-Third Fighter Group in Cap Bon, Tunisia. The Nazi enemy was a mere hundred miles away from them, firmly entrenched on the Italian island of Sicily. The Thirty-Third was commanded by Colonel William "Spike" Momyer, a large, imposing man who made it clear from the moment Davis and Roberts reported that he had little respect for the Ninety-Ninth. He did not stand to greet the men, nor did he return their salutes. He just stated brusquely that he hoped the Ninety-Ninth had replacements because the Thirty-Third had been losing a lot of their squadron commanders.

Within a week of their arrival, the Ninety-Ninth received their first combat mission order. With Sicily firmly in control of the Germans and Italians, American generals decided that it was necessary to capture some of the smaller nearby islands before moving in on Sicily itself. The first of these island targets was Pantelleria. Within a few days of the high command's decision on how to proceed, Davis received orders for the Ninety-Ninth's first mission.

Initial assignments saw the pilots sent out on strafing missions—low-flying bombing runs intended to destroy small targets such as supply storehouses, ammunition vehicles, and buildings that might have been used as temporary headquarters by the enemy. On June 2, four pilots from the Ninety-Ninth—Bill Campbell, Clarence Jamison, Charlie Hall, and James Wiley—jumped into their planes, fired up the engines, and embarked on their first combat as wingmen to the Thirty-Third. Momyer intended to try to embarrass the four men by losing them once they were all airborne, but to his surprise all four fliers stuck right with them.

It became real for the men flying in their first mission when the enemy on the ground began firing antiaircraft weapons at them and they saw the black cloud puffs outside their windows. Everyone returned to the base safely—mission accomplished. The following day Campbell, Jamison, Hall, and Wiley took their own squadron out on the same run. The mission went off without any problems, but Momyer was determined to find a way to undermine the Ninety-Ninth. He even went so far as to change the time of a briefing without informing the Ninety-Ninth members. Going by the original schedule, the men arrived as the briefing was concluding.

Still, the pilots kept their minds on the tasks at hand, unwilling to play Momyer's game. On June 9th, while Clarence Jamison, Charlie Dryden, Spann Watson, Sidney Brooks, Willie Ashley, and Leon Roberts were escorting 12 bombers, they encountered a large contingent of enemy aircraft. Prior to the beginning of the flight missions, escort pilots were ordered never to leave a bomber unprotected to pursue an enemy fighter. If attacked during an escort run, they were ordered to fight off the enemy while staying with the bombers. Eight of the fighter planes followed orders and escorted the bombers home, but four others broke away and went after the Me-109s. The inexperienced pilots may have meant well, but the infraction almost cost the Ninety-Ninth its active battle-ready status.

The Ninety-Ninth participated in several more missions throughout the rest of the month and into July. Pantelleria surrendered on June 11th, and made history in the process. It was the first time enemy territory had been defeated by the use of air power alone. Shortly after Pantelleria fell, the islands of Lampedusa and Limosa followed. With them out of the way, the Allied forces had control of the waters that led to Sicily and Italy itself.

With the focus first on Sicily, the Ninety-Ninth's primary job became escorting bombers on their missions over Sicily. On July 2, members of the Ninety-Ninth joined up with 60 fighter pilots from three white groups as they flew over the Mediterranean to meet up with several bomber planes. As they got closer to their targets, the bombers and fighter planes encountered heavy antiaircraft fire. By the time the bombers had dropped their ordnance, German fighter planes were airborne. The bombers headed back to North Africa, but the enemy engaged Hall, Dryden, Knighten, Campbell, Watson, McCullin, and White.

After several furious minutes of aerial combat, Hall, who was flying his eighth mission, finally saw the enemy close enough to fire upon. He watched as his tracer bullets hit the German fighter plane, which attempted to make a turn, and then suddenly plunged to the ground. Charlie Hall had just

Pilots and crew from the Ninety-Ninth review the day's events at a U.S. airbase in the Mediterranean. The Ninety-Ninth was instrumental in military successes in Italy, but its members still faced colleagues who aimed to undermine their efforts.

scored the downing of an enemy aircraft, the first for the Ninety-Ninth Fighter Squadron. For his kill, Hall earned the Distinguished Flying Cross, the highest commendation awarded by the Air Corps. Even so, the jubilation was overshadowed by the news that McCullin and White failed to return—the Ninety-Ninth squadron's first combat casualties.

With the fall of the smaller islands the Allied forces were able to begin the ground invasion of Sicily in mid-July. The Ninety-Ninth didn't get to see another enemy plane for the next six months, but were kept busy providing essential air support for the troops on the ground, sometimes flying as many as three missions a day. Lou Purnell remembers of this time:

> We'd sit in our aircraft waiting for a red flag to take off, then we'd go up, come down, refuel, and go back up. Some of the guys would make four missions a day. I've talked to other squadrons, and that was unheard of. But if we broke under the pressure, that would have been all they wanted. We were really under a magnifying glass. They reported the least little discrepancy.

The pilots of the Ninety-Ninth suspected that someone was looking for any excuse to discredit them and the whole Tuskegee program. Willie Fuller, a member of the Ninety-Ninth, recalled how a few of the white pilots made disparaging remarks. During one mission on a pretty cloudy day, the pilots of the Ninety-Ninth felt it was too dangerous to continue on to their targets, so they returned to base. All of the white pilots went on the next flight out, took a chance on flying in the overcast skies, and two of their pilots didn't make it back. Despite the losses, the white pilots made sure to mention that the Ninety-Ninth pilots had turned back. Fuller thought it was crazy that while two men were dead, they were being ridiculed for putting safety first.

The average white pilot flew 50 missions before being rotated with a replacement and heading home. Because the replacements for the men of the Ninety-Ninth only came from Tuskegee, they flew as many as 70 missions before they were relieved. The schedule was tough on the pilots, and just as brutal on the ground support crew personnel who had to keep servicing the planes every time they returned from a flight.

By the end of August, the enemy had been defeated in Sicily. In September, Lieutenant Colonel Davis was called back to the United States to take command of the all-black 332nd Fighter Group that consisted of two all-black fighter squadrons—the 100th and the 301st—and the 302nd squadron, an all-black technical support group. With Davis departing, Captain George "Spanky"

Pilots receive their morning briefing in Italy. While most white pilots were permitted to rotate out of combat after 50 missions, the average black pilot had to fly 70. The black pilots were also about to engage in their fiercest battle yet—battling Col. Momyer from keeping the Ninety-Ninth out of commission.

Roberts was named the new Ninety-Ninth squadron commander.

The next offensive planned was against the town of Salerno on the Italian mainland. The idea was to capture enough of the countryside to set up airfields so that planes could leave from these bases to launch an aerial attack on Germany. The Ninety-Ninth was not able to supply air support as their P-40s did not have the range to fly from the base to the invasion point and back to the base. When runways were completed near Paestum, an area just south of Salerno, an officer and some service personnel from the Ninety-Ninth flew out there to prepare the base for the arrival of several squadrons. When the three white squadrons of the Thirty-Third Fighter Group left for Paestum, the rest of the Ninety-Ninth was ordered to stay behind in Sicily.

The event wouldn't have been significant had the Germans not launched a frantic counterattack that sent the Allies scrambling back almost to the beaches of Salerno. All available personnel were ordered into combat. The pilots of the Thirty-Third Fighter Group took to the air and tallied 11 enemy planes shot down when the battle ended a few days later. The Ninety-Ninth had been kept away from the battle lines. Not long after, the reason became clear. Eager to draw attention to the few minor miscues committed by the Ninety-Ninth, Colonel Momyer wrote a negative report about their performance in the hopes of damaging their credibility. He accused the Ninety-Ninth squadron of being undisciplined and disorganized:

> Based on the performance of the 99th Fighter Squadron to date, it is my opinion that they are not of the fighting caliber of any squadron in this group. They have failed to display the aggressiveness and daring for combat that are necessary to be a first class fighting organization. It may be expected that we will get less work and less operational time out of the 99th Fighter Squadron than any squadron in this group.

As his report made its way up through the ranks of the Air Corps, each reviewer added his own negative comments. By the time Momyer's report reached General "Hap" Arnold, the future of the Ninety-Ninth did not look promising.

Arnold sent the report on to the McCloy Committee of the War Department. It was their job to create policy on the use of black soldiers in the military. The report had harsh words about the all-black squadron, including that "the 99th was not aggressive, did not have the will to win or reach an objective, did not have the needed stamina, and could not fight as a team." The report went further in recommending "that all black squadrons be assigned non-combat roles."

The Momyer report and its accusations were what greeted Lieutenant Colonel Davis as he returned to the United States to take command of the 332nd Fighter Group. Understandably angry, Davis felt Momyer's report smelled of racism. Most of the charges listed in the report referenced the first few days of the squadron's new experience in combat. When Davis was ordered to testify before the McCloy Committee, he acknowledged his squadron's mistakes but attributed them to inexperience in combat. He was quick to follow by stating that the mistakes had been addressed, even though that did not appear anywhere in the report.

As for his troops' stamina, Davis was quick to point out that his men had flown for two months straight without replacements and flew as many as three to six missions a day. Though not firmly yet convinced that blacks belonged in fighter planes, the Air Corps and War Department consented to Davis taking the 332nd Fighter Group overseas to join up with the Ninety-Ninth Fighter Squadron after completing training at the end of the year. However, the army did order a study on the Ninety-Ninth entitled "Operations of the 99th Fighter Squadron Compared with Other P-40 Squadrons in the Mediterranean Theater of Operations." The study would be conducted from July 1943 to February 1944, and would assess the pilots' performances based on their flight missions, quickness, the number of enemy casualties, and their own losses.

Half a world away, the men of the Ninety-Ninth—unaware of the controversy back home—received orders on October 17th to move to Foggia, Italy. Dubbed the "Lonely Eagles"—as three fighter squadrons make up a group, and the Ninety-Ninth were a squadron without a group—the Ninety-Ninth was assigned to the Seventy-Ninth Fighter Group as a *fourth* squadron. This proved to be a good move; commanding officer Colonel Earl E. Bates treated the men of the Ninety-Ninth as if they were just as integral to the fighter group as the other squadrons. Ignoring the segregation policy, Bates slowly and unobtrusively began integrating the men of the

Ninety-Ninth with the men of the Seventy-Ninth into all missions.

Flying with the men of the Seventy-Ninth, who were a very proficient combat unit, the pilots of the Ninety-Ninth gained a great deal of experience, which in turn gave the men more confidence in their abilities. Not having encountered any enemy planes for almost three months, the Ninety-Ninth learned better combat flying techniques, including aerial maneuvers and flight formations with the pilots of the Seventy-Ninth.

During the fall months of September and October, the Allied forces captured the towns of Foggia and Naples, as well as the islands of Sardinia and Corsica. The Germans were on a retreat back up the boot-shaped country, while the Allies continued to chase them, and the bombers flew missions destroying bridges, highway, convoys, and depots to cut off enemy supplies and reinforcements. But by November and into the wintry month of December, the rainy, cold weather began hampering combat operations. The good news was that replacements like Bob Deiz, Sam Bruce, Howard Baugh, Clarence Allen, and C. C. "Curtis" Robinson were finally coming overseas.

The Allies planned their next major invasion at Anzio on Italy's west coast just south of Rome. The Ninety-Ninth was released from Bate's group so they could join up with the 324th Fighter Group at Capodicino, south of Anzio. The Battle for Anzio began on January 22, 1944. The Allies hit the beaches and unloaded their tanks and support vehicles, encountering little enemy resistance. The Ninety-Ninth pilots' mission was to fly protective patrols over the Allied ships that were transporting troops and supplies to the beach.

After a few days the Germans started fighting back, firing antiaircraft artillery and swarming the skies with their fighter planes. Most of the time the Allied pilots were outnumbered but still outmaneuvered the enemy aircraft so their gunners couldn't get a clear shot. That changed on the morning of January 27th. It was perhaps the most decisive day for the pilots of the Ninety-Ninth and the entire "experiment."

The historic day began about 8:30 in the morning. Clarence Jamison was flying with about 12 other pilots, including Deiz, Baugh, and Allen, when radar ground control radioed up that enemy planes had been spotted. Within seconds the German planes came screaming down on them. Maneuvering in behind them, Jamison and the others began attacking. Willie Ashley took off after a German 190, blasting his guns until the enemy plane started to smoke and then burst into a ball of fire. Deiz pulled up behind another 190 and fired away. A piece of the aircraft flew off and the plane nose-dived into the ground. Both Baugh and Allen spotted another 190, shooting at it simultaneously. It too dropped straight to the ground, kicking up a cloud of dust as it hit.

While Baugh went after another 190, Leon Roberts was chasing his own. He fired away, hitting the 190 in the wing, and just like the others, it went hurtling toward the earth. Ed Toppins made the last kill of the morning, firing one quick round into another 190 and watching it explode on impact with the ground. Before the attack was over several enemy planes were also damaged. The Ninety-Ninth ground crew watched in disbelief as they saw five planes go into a victory roll (slow roll down near the ground) one at a time as they came back to base. In less time than it takes to take off and reach patrol altitude, five enemy planes were destroyed, and several more damaged.

In the afternoon more of the Ninety-Ninth pilots had successes. Captain Custis led another group of fighter planes into aerial battle against German 190s and Messerschmidt 109s that were flying down from Rome toward Anzio. Before the encounter ended, Custis, Wilson Eagleson, and Charles Bailey had downed three more enemy aircraft. Another act of courage and determination under extreme circumstances that seemed clearly to refute the Momyer report involved Spanky Roberts. He had taken several bursts of fire that damaged his plane's right-side electrical system. As he coaxed his badly damaged airplane homeward, he saw an enemy machine gun nest below. He

Members of the Ninety-Ninth squadron in Anzio, Italy, where they downed eight German planes in one day and four the following day. They hoped that this success would more than prove their worth to the U.S. Air Corps.

emptied the ammunition from his machine guns, destroying the target. Unfortunately, one of Ninety-Ninth planes didn't return to base safely with its pilot. That evening the men of the Ninety-Ninth celebrated their tallied eight kills and saluted their fallen comrade in battle, Lieutenant Samuel Bruce.

As if the previous days' amazing success had not yet completely registered, the Ninety-Ninth went out the next morning and scored more victories. Charlie Hall led a group of fighters up that included Bruce's friend Bob Deiz, Knighten, Robinson, and Graham "Peepsight" Smith. They weren't in the air too long before they encountered a group of Focke-Wulf 190s and 109s.

Hall blasted a 109 out of the sky before locking his sights on a 190, which he also quickly disposed of. In two days Hall had scored three kills. Meanwhile Deiz, with an almost matter-of-fact demeanor, shot down a Focke-Wulf, which "got in his way," as he later put it. Peepsight Smith may have had the most incredible downing by leading his fire into the flight path of a retreating Focke-Wulf.

Incredibly, the Ninety-Ninth had shot down 12 enemy planes in two days of combat action. That was 11 more than they had destroyed in the six months previously. No doubt the news of the Ninety-Ninth's successes would make it back to the War Department. Each pilot savored the performance of the squadron and hoped they had forever silenced the naysayers who believed that blacks couldn't fly in combat.

An armorer checks on the ammunition belt of a P-51. Amazingly, during one of their escort missions, Captain Wendell Pruitt and Gwynne Pierson sank a destroyer using only machine guns.

8

Recognition at Last

"They rose from adversity through competence, courage, commitment, and capacity to serve America on silver wings and to set a standard few will transcend."

—Inscription on statue in Honor Park,
Air Force Academy, Colorado Springs

The day after the pilots of the Ninety-Ninth completed their incredible two-day run of downed enemy aircraft, Major General John Cannon flew over to Capodichino Airfield to congratulate the men in person. Ironically, Cannon was one of the high command officers who had endorsed Momyer's negative report on the squadron. Before leaving, Cannon urged the men to "keep shooting." The Ninety-Ninth happily obliged. Only a few days into the month of February, pilots Elwood Driver, Wilson Eagleson, Leonard Jackson, and Clinton Mills shot down four more German planes.

For the next few months the Ninety-Ninth flew strafing missions to destroy enemy railroad and supply lines as part of Operation Strangle, the Allies' attempt to capture a German occupied mona-stery in Monte Cassino. When the pilots were grounded because of bad weather, they still had much work to do. Ground crews did work to keep the equipment in top shape, overhauling engines, cleaning and recalibrating fighter plane guns, and repairing any external damage to the planes' wings and bodies.

In April the Ninety-Ninth was detached from the Seventy-Ninth and was assigned to another base shortly after the Allies took control of Rome, where they continued to take part in escort and strafing missions. The Ninety-Ninth also got good news from Washington—the results of the study that covered the actions of the squadron from July 1943 to February 1944 were in. The opening statement of the study read, "An examination of the record of the Ninety-Ninth Fighter Squadron reveals no significant general differences between this squadron and the balance of the P-40 squadrons in the Mediterranean theater of operations." Recognized as a "superb tactical fighter unit," the Ninety-Ninth had been vindicated and praised for a job well done.

The results of the study pleased Lieutenant Colonel Davis. He arrived in Italy in February with his newly formed 332nd Fighter Group, but had been kept informed of how well the Ninety-Ninth was performing. When Davis arrived with his 332nd, which was composed of the 100th, the 301st, and the 302nd, they were assigned to the Montecorvino Air Base near Naples, where they joined up with the Twelfth Air Force. At the time of the 332nd's arrival, the results of the War Department study of the Ninety-Ninth had not yet been completed. Instead of being assigned to the more dangerous combat flying missions, the 332nd was relegated to coastal flight patrols, protecting troops and the prized Anzio harbor.

The pilots did, however, receive new combat airplanes—P-39 Aircobras. Smaller than the P-40 and still slower than their enemy counterpart 190s and 109s, the one advantage of the new plane was its more powerful guns. The pilots didn't think much of their "new" planes, as they were actually hand-me-downs from Russia and England and didn't fly very well. For three months the pilots saw very little aerial combat action since the German planes were so much faster and easily evaded attack.

The role of the 332nd in the war changed when General Ira Eaker, commander of the Fifteenth Air Force, approached Davis's group for combat assistance. Eaker had been sending his bombers to northern France and into Germany to obliterate enemy supply lines, munitions and equipment factories, and any other enemy targets on the ground. By now the Ninety-Ninth had been exonerated by the study results, and the 332nd was getting its own share of praise. Eaker had a problem, and realized that the men of the 332nd could help. He was losing American bombers at a horrendous rate. In February alone, 114 bombers and 1,000 crewmen had been lost during raids against the enemy. Eaker had lost more than 300 men in just one bombing raid over the oil fields of Ploesti (Romania), and suffered the loss of 600 soldiers and 60 bombers in a single raid over Germany.

Part of the problem was that the British Spitfire escort planes did not have the range to escort the bombers very far, which left them like sitting ducks against the attacking German Messerschmidts. Eaker knew of the 332nd's escort record and wanted them to protect his planes. Davis saw this as a tremendous opportunity for his men and agreed.

On May 31st, the 332nd was reassigned to the Fifteenth Strategic Air Force. A few days later they headed to Ramatelli, closer to where the combat action was taking place. The pilots again got new planes to fly—the Republic P-47 Thunderjet. It was nicknamed "the Jug" because it was a heavy plane—some of the pilots joked that flying the P-47 was like trying to fly a bathtub. But they had .50 caliber machine guns, 500-pound bomb loads, and could "take a beating." The men jazzed up "the Jug" by painting its tail red. Soon the planes became known as "Red Tails."

The Tuskegee Airmen monument in Walterboro, S.C., shows the distinctive "Red Tail" paint applied to the P-47s of the 332nd.

Though P-47s didn't have the range to escort the bombers on long-range bombing missions, the pilots had other plans. Two newer, faster, long-range fighter planes were ushered into service—the P-38 and the P-51. German pilots knew that those planes would be used to escort the bombers deep into enemy territory, but also knew that the bombers would have little or no short-range escort protection going out from their bases. The belief was that the German fighters would try to attack the bombers while they were without escort fliers closer to their bases. One-Hundredth squadron leader Melvin "Red" Jackson decided to surprise the enemy by having pilots of the 332nd escort the bombers as far as they could. If the enemy came close, they'd engage them in battle.

Jackson's hunch paid off. Not long after takeoff, the P-47 pilots spotted more than two dozen German 109s heading for the bombers. Moments later Jackson heard Commander Davis yell "Go get 'em" and the aerial battle was on. Wendell Pruitt, one of the most popular guys of the 302nd squadron, recorded the first enemy kill. Frederick Funderberg of the 301st fired at a 109 and watched it explode. The 332nd had five victories in all that day. Davis would be awarded the Distinguished Flying Cross for his outstanding leadership during the mission. But the day's good work came at a price—pilot Cornelius Rogers didn't make it back to base.

The amazing feats of the 332nd kept coming. Near the end of June, while returning from a strafing run over Yugoslavia, five Red Tails spotted a German naval destroyer in the waters near Trieste, along the Adriatic coast. Despite not having any bombs, the pilots attacked the ship using only their .50 caliber machine guns. Captain Wendell Pruitt's bullets set the ship on fire, and Gwynne Pierson finished the job when his machine gun fire apparently hit a cache of weapons, causing the vessel to explode and sink. It was the first time an enemy vessel had been destroyed by gunfire. Both Pruitt and Pierson were awarded the Distinguished Flying Cross for their accomplishment. It was the 332nd's last hoorah in the "Jugs," but the 332nd Fighter Group would make more history before the war's end.

The Tuskegee Airmen have the distinction of flying more types of planes than any other unit in the history of the military. With the arrival of new planes in June 1944—the P-51 Mustang—the men of the 332nd would be flying their fourth fighter aircraft.

The P-51 Mustang was by far the most superior yet. Pilot Walter Palmer of the 100th said, "If the P-39 was a VW and the P-47 a Buick, the P-51 was the Cadillac of fighters with a Rolls Royce engine." With its larger gas tanks, the P-51 could fly farther than the other P-class planes, and could handle higher altitudes like the B-17 bombers they escorted. Another member of the 100th squadron, Woodrow Crockett, called it a "dream plane."

The P-51 could climb, turn, fly low, and was great for strafing missions. The cockpit was larger than the other P-class planes, so the taller, bigger guys finally had an aircraft that was comfortable to fly on a several-hour mission. The ground crews took great pride in painting the now-familiar red on the new aircraft tails. The Tuskegee pilots wanted the American bomber pilots and crews to know who was escorting them when they looked out the window. Some of the bombers dubbed them the "Red Tail Angels" because they knew if they were being escorted by the Red Tails, they would never be left behind by fighter pilots who would go off to score kills for their own records. The 332nd would distinguish themselves from all the other escort pilot fighter groups as being the only group in the United States armed forces that never lost a bomber to enemy fire.

Because the Ninety-Ninth squadron had flown so many missions without a break or replacements and were showing signs of severe exhaustion and battle fatigue, the 332nd flight surgeon grounded them. The other pilots of the 332nd took the P-51s on practice flights until they got used to handling the new plane. The 332nd had two main objectives: to protect bombers while they were airborne destroying enemy locations, and to soften up the enemy entrenched along the French southern coast until the massive Allied invasion scheduled for mid-August.

In July, some of the 332nd squadron began flying several bomber escort missions to enemy airfields, oil depots, vehicle factories, submarine harbors, bridges, and radar stations. The *only* objective was to protect the bombers. Davis and Eaker didn't care if the Red Tails never shot down another enemy plane.

However, if the opportunity presented itself, the men were not discouraged from doing so. While on an escort mission on July 12th in heavy cloud cover, the Red Tails sighted several enemy fighters moving in to attack bomber planes. Without leaving the bombers unprotected, the fighter pilots attacked the fleeing enemy. Captain Elsberry scored three kills.

By the end of July, the 332nd had tallied up 38 enemy planes shot out of the sky in just over a 12-day period. The Red Tails also contributed to the destruction of much of the enemy's fuel storage depots, which accounted for the loss of about 400 million gallons of fuel. Without the desperately needed fuel, enemy planes, tanks, and other vehicles sat idle, leaving them easy targets for destruction. With fewer enemy planes able to get airborne—some sent back to Germany to protect the homeland, and others dodging the Allied fighter pilots—it became more difficult to shoot down enemy aircraft.

Over the next several months, the 332nd flew strafing missions, destroying anything "enemy-looking"—airfields, parked planes, tanks, and convoys. By the end of 1944, the Red Tails' statistics were staggering: 62 enemy planes shot down, and countless enemy targets on the ground demolished beyond recognition.

Despite suffering such staggering losses, the Germans weren't capitulating. In fact, they were ready to introduce a new jet aircraft, the Messerschmitt 262 (Me-262), that could outfly and outmaneuver most of the Allies' planes. It wasn't until sometime in December that anyone from the 332nd got a look at the Me-262. It was fast—capable of speeds in excess of 500 miles per hour. Fortunately for the Allies, the jets were completed about two years too late. Still, while it appeared Allied victory in the war was imminent, the Germans put the Me-262 and its sister, Me-163, up in the air. Realizing that though the new planes would not turn the tide of the war against the Allies but could certainly drag it out, the high command decided to bomb the German airplane factories. It had long been decided that whenever any Fifteenth Air Force bombers flew on a mission, the 332nd would be right by their wings.

Capt. Andrew Turner prepares to escort a heavy bomber. In 200 escort missions during the war, no Red Tail escort ever lost a bomber. Yet such outstanding achievements did not earn official respect and recognition until long after the war ended.

Toward the end of March, Colonel Davis led his 332nd Fighter Group on a 1,600-mile round-trip escort mission for B-17s flying to Berlin. Though they were supposed to hand off the final leg of the escort to another fighter group, the group never showed—so Davis and his men stayed with the bombers.

The 332nd pilots encountered the Me-262s and Me-163s for the first time, but the German pilots were inexperienced in flying the new jets, and the Red Tails held firm without losing a single bomber. They did suffer their own casualties, however, with the loss of three Red Tail members. For their tenacity and protection in the mission, the 332nd Fighter Group was awarded the Distinguished Unit Citation.

A few more battles followed with the Red Tails accounting for 13 downed Me-262s before word got to the front that President Franklin Roosevelt had died on April 12th, making Vice President Harry S. Truman president. On April 26th, Allied planes shot down the last planes in Europe of World War II, the same day Nazi leader Adolf Hitler took his own life. Taking part in the aerial battle were the pilots of the 301st, who were credited with four kills. The 332nd flew its final mission in 1945 on the last day of April. Germany surrendered on May 8th, and by June, many of the Red Tail pilots were on their way home.

Since Japan had not yet surrendered, the Red Tails wondered if they'd be sent to fight in the Pacific. Colonel Davis took command of the 477th Composite Group, which was made up of two bombardment squadrons, including the Ninety-Ninth and the 100th Fighter Squadrons. The 477th began intensive training in anticipation of seeing duty in the Pacific theater. However, the war ended before they could be dispatched. Two atomic bombs were dropped on the Japanese cities of Hiroshima and Nagasaki, forcing an unconditional surrender on August 14th. World War II was officially over.

The Tuskegee Airmen's legacy is twofold. Their combat record alone is amazing. From the time of their first mission to their last combat flight, the Ninety-Ninth and the 332nd flew 1,578 missions including more than 15,000 sorties. They sent 450 pilots into battle, 66 of whom died. Thirty-two of the Red Tails who were downed alive became POWs. They sank one enemy destroyer; shot down more than 100 German planes, and destroyed countless railcars, trucks, tanks, and other vehicles.

One hundred fifty Distinguished Flying Crosses, 744 Air Medals, 8 Purple Hearts, and 14 Bronze Stars were awarded among the men. Perhaps the most important statistic of all was the number of Allied bombers lost to enemy fighters under the Red Tails' escort—zero.

Despite their heroic performance, the Tuskegee Airmen continued to be subjected to racism when they came home. The military continued its policy of segregating the blacks from the whites. President Harry S. Truman finally put an end to that. He asked how a country built on freedom for all, with equal protections under the law, could continue to discriminate against its own. On July 26, 1948, Truman issued Executive Order 9981 that stated in part:

> It is hereby declared to be the policy of the President that there shall be equality of treatment and opportunity for all persons in the armed services without regard to race, color, religion, or national origin. This policy shall be put into effect as rapidly as possible, having due regard to the time required to effectuate any necessary changes without impairing efficiency or morale.

Many believe that it was the courage, determination, and success demonstrated by the men who came out of the "Tuskegee Experiment" that was the catalyst in bringing an end to the racial barriers and segregation in the United States armed forces. Their unbreakable spirit in the face of strong opposition helped pave the way for future American black military patriots like former general and current secretary of state Colin Powell and the veterans of Korea, Vietnam, the Persian Gulf War, and Operation Enduring Freedom. They also opened the skies high above earth for men like astronauts Guion Bluford (USAF), Frederick Gregory (USAF), and Charles Bolden (USMC).

Like the all-Japanese American 442nd Regiment and the Native American Code Talkers of World War II, national recognition came slow to the Tuskegee Airmen. Today, the accomplishments

President Bill Clinton pins a fourth star to the shoulder of Lt. Col. Davis Jr. during a 1998 ceremony honoring his military service—28 years after Davis retired. The Tuskegee Airmen have garnered belated recognition for their achievements in recent years, including a film made about them in 1996.

of the Tuskegee Airmen are celebrated all over America. There is a Tuskegee Airmen museum in Detroit, Michigan; a monument honoring the men stands tall at the Air Force Museum in Dayton, Ohio; a Tuskegee Airmen exhibit at the Smithsonian Air and Space Museum in Washington, DC; and a statue in Honor Park on the grounds of the Air Force Academy in Colorado Springs, Colorado. The granite monument reads: "To the Tuskegee Airmen, valiant men and women, who during World War II participated in the Tuskegee experience; and yet despite staggering odds rendered outstanding military service to the United States of America."

1939 **May** Members of the National Airman's Association, an organization comprised of black pilots, meet with Senator Harry S. Truman from Missouri to discuss initiating Civilian Pilot Training Programs for blacks.

1940 **December** The Army Air Corps submits a proposal to the War Department to form an all-black fighter squadron. It is later dubbed the "Tuskegee Experiment."

1941 **January 16** The Ninety-Ninth Pursuit Squadron is established by the War Department. The location for training is Tuskegee, Alabama. Base construction of the Tuskegee Army Air Field is awarded to a black architectural firm, McKissack and McKissack, Inc.

July 19 Tuskegee Army Air Field officially opens.

September 2 Captain Benjamin O. Davis Jr. is the first black American to fly an aircraft solo as an officer in the U.S. Army Air Corps.

December 7 The Japanese bomb Pearl Harbor. The next day the United States enters World War II.

1942 **March 1** Captain Benjamin O. Davis Jr. is promoted to Lt. Colonel.

March 6 Benjamin O. Davis Jr., Lemuel Custis, Mac Ross, George Roberts, and Charles DeBow graduate and earn their wings as members of the first class of Tuskegee pilots.

May 15 The 100th Fighter Squadron is activated as a part of the creation of the 332nd Fighter Group.

August 24 Lt. Colonel Benjamin Davis Jr. takes command of the Ninety-Ninth Fighter Squadron.

1943 **April 15** Having received combat orders, the Ninety-Ninth Fighter Squadron is sent to North Africa.

May 31 The Ninety-Ninth Fighter Squadron arrives at Farjouna, Cape Bon, South Tunis, to begin combat missions as part of the Thirty-Third Fighter Group.

July 2 Captain Charles B. Hall is the first black pilot to shoot down an enemy aircraft.

August Lt. Colonel Davis Jr. returns to the United States to command the 332nd Fighter Group. The 332nd is comprised of the all-black 100th, 301st, and 302nd Fighter Squadrons. George Roberts takes over command of the Ninety-Ninth.

September Col. William Momyer writes a negative report on the Ninety-Ninth.

October 7 The Ninety-Ninth is attached to the Seventy-Ninth Fighter Group of the Twelfth Air Force.

October 16 Lt. Colonel Davis Jr. testifies before the McCloy Committee to address the charges in the Momyer report.

1944   **January** Lt. Colonel Davis Jr. and the 332nd arrive in Taranto, Italy, and are attached to the Twelfth Air Force.

January 27 Members of the Ninety-Ninth engage German enemy aircraft, shooting down eight planes in one day.

June 25 Pilots of the 302nd Fighter Squadron sink a German destroyer using only machine gunfire from their P-47s.

June The 332nd becomes part of the Fifteenth Air Force. The Ninety-Ninth Fighter Squadron is added to the 332nd Fighter Group as its fourth squadron.

August The 332nd joins in the invasion of southern France, escorting bombers and taking part in ground attack missions in Romania and Czechoslovakia.

September 10 Four pilots of the 332nd—Benjamin O. Davis Jr., Clarence Lester, Jack Holsclaw, and Joseph Elsberry—are awarded the Distinguished Flying Cross.

1945   **March 15** The all-black 477th Bombardment Group is moved from Godman Field, Kentucky, to Freeman Field, Indiana.

April 1 The men of the 477th protest the strict segregation policies in a document called Regulation 85-2 that was ordered by base commander Colonel Robert Selway.

April 5 Several black pilots led by 2nd Lt. Roger C. Terry and Lt. Marsden Thompson attempt to enter the segregated officers' club. Sixty-nine black officers are arrested.

April 9 Col. Robert Selway orders the black officers to sign a statement acknowledging that they have read and accept Regulation 85-2. The officers, 101 in all, refuse. In what was later called the "Freeman Field Incident," all but three of the officers are released.

June Col. Benjamin O. Davis Jr. is named commander of the 477th Composite Group, which includes the Ninety-Ninth and 100th Fighter Squadrons. They begin to train for combat in the Pacific theater.

August 14 World War II ends with the surrender of Japan.

1948   **July 26** President Harry S. Truman issues Executive Order 9981 desegregating the armed forces.

1954   **October 27** Col. Davis Jr. is promoted to brigadier general, becoming the first African-American to wear one star in the United States Air Force.

1995   **August 12** The air force clears the service records of all Tuskegee Airmen who took part in the "Freeman Field Incident," vindicating their stand for equality.

2002   **July** Brigadier General Davis Jr. dies.

Buckley, Gail Lumet. *American Patriots: The Story of Blacks in the Military from the Revolution to Desert Storm.* New York: Random House, 2001.

George, Linda and Charles George. *The Tuskegee Airmen (Cornerstones of Freedom).* Connecticut: Children's Press, 2000.

Harris, Jacqueline. *The Tuskegee Airmen: Black Heroes of World War II.* Parsippany, New Jersey: Dillon Press, 1996.

Hart, Philip S. and Reeve Lindbergh. *Flying Free: America's First Black Aviators.* Minneapolis, Minnesota: Lerner Publications Company, 1996.

Holman, Lynn and Thomas Reilly. *Black Knights: The Story of the Tuskegee Airmen.* Gretna, Louisiana: Pelican Publishing Company, 2001.

Holway, John B. *Red Tails, Black Wings: The Men of America's Black Air Force.* Las Cruces, New Mexico: Yucca Tree Press, 1997.

McKissack, Patricia and Fredrick McKissack. *Red-Tail Angels: The Story of the Tuskegee Airmen of World War II.* New York: Walker and Company, 1995.

George, Linda and Charles George. *The Tuskegee Airmen (Cornerstones of Freedom)*. Connecticut: Children's Press, 2000.

Hart, Philip S. and Reeve Lindbergh. *Flying Free: America's First Black Aviators*. Minneapolis, Minnesota: Lerner Publications Company, 1996.

Holman, Lynn and Thomas Reilly. *Black Knights: The Story of the Tuskegee Airmen*. Gretna, Louisiana: Pelican Publishing Company, 2001.

McKissack, Patricia and Fredrick McKissack. *Red-Tail Angels: The Story of the Tuskegee Airmen of World War II*. New York: Walker and Company, 1995.

http://tuskegeeairmen.org/
[Tuskegee Airmen Inc.]

http://www.tuskegee.com/theairmen.html
[The Tuskegee Airmen Story]

http://160.111.252.56/nasm/blackwings/index.html
[Black Wings: African American Pioneer Aviators]

http://www.military.com/Content/MoreContent1/?file=BH_Tuskegee7
[Military.com: Black History Month]

http://www.lindberghfoundation.org/
[Charles and Ann Morrow Lindbergh Foundation]

http://www.naacp.org/
[NAACP official website]

page:

2: The National Archives
NWDNS-44-PA-1217

6: © Corbis

11: © Bettmann/Corbis

13: Hulton Archive/Getty Images

16: © Bettmann/Corbis

18: © Bettmann/Corbis

22: © Bettmann/Corbis

27: AP, Wide World Photos

30: Hulton Archive/Getty Images

35: Hulton Archive/Getty Images

36: © The Mariners' Museum/Corbis

38: The National Archives
NWDNS-208-NP-6BBB

43: AP, Wide World Photos

44: © Bettmann/Corbis

46: AP, Wide World Photos

50: The National Archives
NWDNS-208-MO-120H-29054

53: AP, Wide World Photos

55: The National Archives
NWDNS-208-VM-1-5-69G

58: The National Archives
NWDNS-208-NP-5QQ-3

62: AP, Wide World Photos

67: AP, Wide World Photos

70: The National Archives
NWDS-208-AA-49E-1-1

72: The National Archives
NWDNS-111-SC-184968

77: The National Archives
NWDNS-208-N-32987

79: The National Archives
NWDNS-208-N-32987

84: The National Archives
NWDNS-80-G-54413

86: The National Archives
NWDNS-208-MO-18H-32984

90: AP, Wide World Photos

94: The National Archives
NWDNS-MO-18K-32981

97: AP, Wide World Photos

Cover: © Bettmann/Corbis

Judy L. Hasday, a native of Pennsylvania, received her B.A. in communications and her Ed.M. in instructional technologies from Temple University. Ms. Hasday has written many books for young adults, including an award-winning biography of James Earl Jones, and *Extraordinary Women Athletes,* a National Social Studies Council "2001 Notable Social Studies Trade Book for Young People."